PUFFIN BOOKS

THE PUFFIN BOOK OF CAR GAMES

Long car journeys can be boring, hot, and tiring and it helps if you know lots of games to play that will keep your mind (or your fingers) occupied. There are over a hundred car games, none of which needs anything more complex than a box of matches, a map, a pencil, or a piece of paper.

Test your memory with *Did you see?*; close your eyes and guess an object from the sound it makes; play football with pedestrian crossings and billiards with bus-stops, or try poker with car number-plates. You can do a census count or be a navigator, keep a log book or a holiday journal, and even be a tourist courier. If you get stuck in traffic jams there are lots of things you can do – finger-miming, balancing tricks, road-map games, and pencil-and-paper word and number games. There's singing too, and paper folding, and, when it gets dark, games specially designed to send you to sleep so that the driver gets a break!

The Puffin Book of Car Games also includes games you can play outside the car, when you stop for a picnic, perhaps, or when you are spending a day on the beach. In fact, not only is it a book to make the going great – it will also help you enjoy being there!

D1137529

M Spittles

Ben Spittles book.

THE PUFFIN BOOK OF
CAR GAMES

D. St P. BARNARD

Illustrated by Nigel Paige

PUFFIN BOOKS

PUFFIN BOOKS

Published by the Penguin Group
27 Wrights Lane, London w8 5tz, England
Viking Penguin Inc., 40 West 23rd Street, New York, New York 10010, USA
Penguin Books Australia Ltd, Ringwood, Victoria, Australia
Penguin Books Canada Ltd, 2801 John Street, Markham, Ontario, Canada l3r 1b4
Penguin Books (NZ) Ltd, 182–190 Wairau Road, Auckland 10, New Zealand

Penguin Books Ltd, Registered Offices: Harmondsworth, Middlesex, England

First published 1977
7 9 10 8

Made and printed in Great Britain by
Richard Clay Ltd, Bungay, Suffolk
Set in Monotype Baskerville

Contents

Introduction

The games in this book need virtually no equipment, as most of them can be played with scraps of paper, or the odds and ends which are usually to hand on a car journey. Some of the games call for nothing other than nimble wits or nimble fingers.

But if you are planning a long journey or holiday, there is no reason why you should not take along with you a few 'optional extras' – writing paper for instance. The margin of a newspaper or the back of a used envelope is good enough for scribbling or scoring, but a few sheets of proper writing paper or drawing paper are very useful – especially if you want to sketch things or draw largish diagrams.

The most convenient way to carry paper is on a clipboard. A piece of heavy cardboard (or preferably hardboard) about 15 inches long by 10 inches wide, with a large bulldog clip at the top, makes an ideal clipboard. Slip a dozen or so sheets of paper under the bulldog clip, and the board gives you something flat and firm to write on. If you bore a small hole in one corner of the board, you can tie on a pencil, so that it is always readily to hand – and if the pencil has a rubber on the end, so much the better.

Short, stubby pencils are usually most convenient – and don't oversharpen them if you intend using them in a car. Too sharp a point could be dangerous if the car were to give a sudden lurch. Crayons or felt-tipped pens are safer, and more fun too.

A few paper clips, some rubber bands, a small roll of sticky-tape and a ball of string all have their uses. And if you like cutting things out, or are thinking of making a scrapbook of the journey, a pair of scissors may prove handy. On no account use scissors in the back of a moving vehicle, because anything sharp is potentially dangerous in a car.

A box of matches is a must – not just for lighting a camp fire, but also for playing match games, and for scoring other games as well. Claiming one match from the box for each point scored in a game is both easier and more rewarding than entering numbers on a sheet of paper. Also the final tally is less open to dispute.

Buttons can also be used for scoring purposes, and if some are white and some are black, they can also be used as counters or pieces for improvised board games.

Playing-cards and board games such as *Ludo* or *Monopoly* are not particularly suitable for the back seat of a car, but they can be played during holiday evenings. On the other hand, portable chess sets can be used even when travelling, as can magnetic draughts.

For outdoor games, a length of light rope can be used for anything from a skipping-rope to an improvised tennis 'net', and is also useful for marking out circles on the sand: one person holds one end in the centre of the proposed circle, and another walks around, holding the rope at a convenient stretch, scratching out the circle as he goes.

When it comes to ball games, practically any sort of ball will do for most holiday sports. Admittedly, a cricket ball, although quite adequate for beach golf, is not much good for tennis, but a tennis ball will do for cricket. A large beach ball is best for most games that involve throwing and catching, but if you don't happen to have a ball with you you will find two or three suggestions for improvising balls on page 165. In fact, throughout the book you will also find suggestions for

14

improvising other items of equipment like nets and goal-posts.

Pieces of wood or rolled-up batons of newspaper can be used for games which involve striking balls, but do take along an old cricket bat and a couple of tennis rackets if you happen to have them – especially if you are keen on that sort of game.

There are more specialized pieces of equipment you could take if they happen to be in the house. A stop-watch, for instance, can add to the fun of timing races and other competitions involving speed, and there are other uses to which it can be put too. On the open road it can be used for guessing games such as estimating how long it will take to pass half a dozen telephone poles, or how long it will take an approaching vehicle to reach one's own car.

And for those who like to know where they are or where they are going, a compass will be invaluable.

If you enjoy sightseeing, a pair of binoculars adds to the fun. Or, if you like examining plants, rocks, or pond-life, a magnifying glass will come in handy. You may go in for collecting things, in which case remember to take along some glass or plastic jars, cardboard boxes, or polythene bags for your specimens. If you take glass jars, wrap them in pieces of old rag to prevent them knocking against each other or against other hard objects.

A small selection of books, magazines, or comics will help to while away breaks on the journey, or on wet afternoons. And for those who like music, a cassette-recorder can add considerably to the party.

Above all, don't forget a notebook for jotting down place-names, telephone numbers, bus times, points of interest – or the hundred and one other things you may wish to record. And an atlas, map, or guide book to the area you are visiting will come in particularly useful.

As I have already said, few of these things are necessary for playing the games in this book, but they can add to the enjoyment – so long as they don't clutter up the car too much. Except for those things that will be required on the journey, stow away your gear in an old overnight bag which can be carried in the boot.

One final, and most important point to remember when it comes to car games, is to make quite sure that, whatever game you are playing, nothing is done that may interfere with the driver when the car is in motion. There are some games (such as *All Change* on page 32) in which the driver can safely take part if he wishes to do so, but he should not be involved in any activity that requires him to take his eye from the road, even momentarily.

Enough said! Let us get on with the games.

Metric Conversion

1 inch	= 2·5 cm
1 foot	= 30·5 cm
1 yard	= 0·91 m
1 mile	= 1·6 km
1 pint	= 6 decilitres
1 gallon	= 4·5 litres
1 m.p.h.	= 1·6 k.p.h.

PART ONE:
TRAFFIC DIVERSIONS

Games and competitions inspired by
motoring

The Passing Scene

Scavenger

The simplest, and possibly the oldest, of all car games is *Scavenger*, and it remains a perennial favourite, especially with younger children.

Make up a list of some ten or twelve objects likely to be encountered during the journey, e.g.:

(a) A chemist's shop   (f) A brown cow
(b) A red bus   (g) A suitcase
(c) A dog on a lead   (h) An aeroplane
(d) A church steeple   (i) A cloth cap
(e) A 'No Entry' sign   (j) An umbrella

The items chosen should be appropriate for both the locality and the time of year. The list is read out, and contestants must scavenge the countryside with their eyes in an attempt to spot the items. They may be spotted in any order, and the list may be referred to from time to time if anyone wishes to refresh his memory.

When someone spots an item it is crossed off the list, and the spotter is awarded one point. When all the items have been spotted, the winner is the one who has accumulated most points.

I Spied

The game of *I Spy* is so venerable and well known that it needs no description. It can of course be played in a car, but you may be more amused by a variation called *I Spied*, which refers to roadside objects that may no longer be in sight by the time contestants have guessed their identity.

One player privately decides upon some roadside object actually visible from the car, and announces 'I just spied with my roving eye something beginning with L' (or whichever letter begins the name of the object).

In the likely event of no one being able to guess the identity of the object immediately, the players may then take turns at asking questions which can be answered by a simple 'Yes' or 'No'. For example, 'Was it on wheels?', 'Can you still see it?'

And if the answers to these questions happen to be 'No':

'Did it have legs?'

A question such as 'How many legs did it have?' is not permitted, because that would require an answer other than 'Yes' or 'No'. The question should be rephrased in the form 'Did it have two legs?'

The answer 'Yes' to this may produce wild guesses such as 'Was it a postman?' or 'Was it a boy?' But experienced guessers will probably prefer to narrow the field of search more cunningly with a question such as 'Did it move?' (After all, it could have been a window-cleaner's ladder!)

The contestant who finally guesses the identity of the object is entitled to spy the next roadside item to be guessed.

If after twenty questions no one has correctly identified the object, the spotter can disclose the answer and choose another object for the next round. If the second object is again not guessed, he is not allowed to spy a third object. The turn passes to the person who has had fewest opportunities to play the role of 'spy'.

Snap

Each contestant decides upon some particular make and colour of car which he intends to look out for, and announces his choice, e.g. 'A red Jaguar' or 'A grey Morris'. As soon as a player spots a car fitting the description he has given he calls 'Snap', and is awarded one point as the winner of that round. Only cars that come into sight after a choice has been made can count for a 'snap'.

On the completion of a round, players have the

option of either sticking to their previous choices, or changing to some other make and colour of car for the next round.

The winner is the player who accumulates most points in the course of five rounds.

Shopping Spree

In this spotting game each of the players makes a list of five items he or she proposes 'buying', e.g.:

(a) A tube of toothpaste (d) A pair of shoes
(b) A pound of steak   (e) A second-hand car
(c) A postage stamp

Now they must keep a look-out for shops or business establishments that can supply these needs. The above list, for instance, could be filled by spotting a chemist's, a butcher's, a post office, a shoe shop, and a car mart.

On spotting the appropriate business, the player calls
'Ding-a-ling' to represent the bell of a cash register, and
crosses the item 'bought' off his list. The items may be
bought in any order, *but only one item can be claimed for*

any one shop. So, if a player has both a box of matches
and a newspaper on his list, he can claim only one of
these items if he spots a newsagent who carries both
these lines.

If two or more contestants are looking for the same
sort of shop, the 'purchase' can be claimed only by the
one who first says 'Ding-a-ling'.

The player who first manages to 'fill his basket' by
buying all five items on his list is the winner.

Travelling Zoo

The idea of this game is for competitors to stock a zoo
with as large a variety as possible of animals, birds,
reptiles, or other creatures that might conceivably be
found in a zoo.

To catch a specimen one must spot some roadside
object the name of which begins with the same letter
as that of the animal claimed. For instance, on spotting
a policeman, one could claim to have caught a panther,
since both the words 'policeman' and 'panther' begin
with the same letter.

Once an object has been claimed as an animal it cannot be used again for another specimen, either by the claimant or by any other zoologist. If a second policeman should heave into view, he cannot be called

a parrot, because policemen have already been declared to be panthers. The 'parrot'-spotter must wait until he sees something else beginning with p – and that shouldn't be too difficult if anyone is walking along the road!

The winner is the zoologist who manages to make the biggest collection of specimens in the space of, say, twenty minutes or half an hour.

A Stands for Auto

This could be played as a competition, with each contestant spotting his own objects, but it is just as much fun played as a cooperative effort with the whole party keeping watch for the next object to be spotted.

The aim is to go through the alphabet from A to Z spotting roadside objects which start with each letter of the alphabet *in proper sequence*. Thus, if the team has already got *a* for automobile, they cannot claim *c* for a constable unless something starting with *b* (e.g. a butcher's) has already been spotted and named.

X is the only letter likely to prove intractable, since very few xylophones, xebecs, or identifiable xenophobes

are left lying about the road. The fairest thing to do is therefore to allow anything starting with 'Ex . . .' as a legitimate substitute for X.

The initial letters of names on signposts, streets, shops, and advertising posters are permitted.

Constantinople

In the old parlour game of *Constantinople* the object was to see how many different words one could make out of the letters of some given word. The game got its name because 'Constantinople' was so often suggested as the word to work on. Actually 'Constantinople' is rather too long for the purpose – one could go on for hours finding new words from its fourteen letters.

It is better to let the next signpost, or the destination-plate of the next bus you see, choose the word for you.

Everyone will need pencil and paper to jot down the words they make up from the name on the signpost or destination-plate.

It is surprising how many words can sometimes be found in quite short names like, for instance, Derby – which gives dry, dye, red, Rye, Ryde, bed, by, bye, byre, bey, and bred.

When it comes to scoring, each ordinary word counts as one point, but any place-name which is found counts as three points, i.e., the above list would score fifteen points, because Rye and Ryde are both place-names (scoring three points each).

The winner of the competition is the player who manages to score most points in five (or ten) minutes.

The Road to Tipperary

This is a team effort. The party decides upon a destination anywhere in the world, preferably some place with at least eight or nine letters in its name.

The aim is to spell out the chosen destination by spotting the letters of its name on signposts. The letters must be spotted *in their correct order*. Thus, if Tipperary is the destination chosen, it could be spelt by spotting the letters (shown in heavy black type) from signposts reading **St**aines, **P**op**l**ar, K**e**w, **R**e**a**ding, and Coven**try**.

Two or more letters may be claimed from a single signpost, provided the letters appear in their correct order, i.e. *t* and *i* can both be claimed from Staines because they appear in that order in the name. But only the *t* could be claimed from a name like Linton, because the *t* of Tipperary must be spotted before the *i*.

Grand Tour

Another game based on signpost names. One member of the party is appointed to keep an eye out for the next signpost and read its name. The party then tries to think up as quickly as possible some country, town, or other geographical locality beginning with the same initial as each of the letters in the name spotted – taking the letters in their proper order.

For instance, if the name spotted were Cromer, the 'tour' could be completed by naming Calcutta, Riviera, Ostend, Maryland, Essen, Rome. Once a place-name has been used, it may not be used again, even if the same letter should crop up a second or third time. For instance, since Riviera was assigned to the first *r* in Cromer, it could not be used again for the final *r* – hence Rome.

An amusing variation of this game is to assign one letter of the name spotted to each member of the party. In the case of Cromer, the first player would take *c*, the second player *r*, and so on. Each player must then think up a business excursion which includes:

(a) The name of some country or town;
(b) The means of transport;
(c) The object of the visit (described by a verb, an adjective, and a noun),

each of which items must begin with the letter that he has been assigned. For instance, the person who has been assigned *c* could announce his excursion by saying 'I am going to Cairo – on a Cow – to Catch Commuting Caterpillars.'

It does not matter how ridiculous the statement is – the sillier it is, the more fun.

28

Did You See?

This is a test of memory which begins with one player pointing out an object on or near the road, and mentioning one feature about it. For example:
'Did you see that traffic warden with two legs?'

The next player must then repeat the remark, linking to it an observation of his own. For example:
'Did you see that traffic warden with two legs, sitting on the bicycle lying on its side?'

To this list, the third contestant adds a further observation, such as:
'Did you see that traffic warden with two legs, sitting on the bicycle lying on its side, behind the lady wheeling a pram?'

The game continues in this way, all players keeping their ears open for possible errors in the recital. If at any point it is generally agreed that a player has made a mistake, he is permitted one more attempt at getting it right. If he fails again, he must drop out.

The winner is the last person remaining in the game when all others have been eliminated by reciting errors.

To avoid arguments, an adjudicator could take brief notes of each object named, but there is really no need to take the game that seriously. It is just as much fun to let the whole project dissolve in a welter of confusion and laughter at the suggestion of traffic wardens lying on their sides in prams being pushed by ladies riding bicycles on two legs.

Blind Man's Journey

Many objects on the road produce sounds by which they may be identified, and the echo of one's own vehicle can sometimes give a clue as to what is being passed. Not only do buses, motorcycles, and railway trains make noises of their own, but bridges, road-cuttings, and high brick walls all produce identifiable echoes.

In *Blind Man's Journey* the idea is for one of the passengers to close his eyes, and see how accurately he can describe the passing scene, relying entirely upon the noises he can hear. The rest of the passengers act as a panel of adjudicators, commenting on how accurate or not are the 'blind man's' observations.

Since most passengers are anxious to try their skill at this game, each spell of being the blind man should be limited to three or four minutes.

Say When

This is another 'blind' game, but here the object is somewhat different than in *Blind Man's Journey*. In *Say When*, the player selects and points out some object (such as a roadsign, conspicuous tree, or motorway bridge) situated a quarter of a mile or so ahead. He then closes his eyes and tries to estimate when the car is abreast of the chosen object.

When he thinks the object has been reached he should say 'When' and open his eyes. His guess counts as a 'hit' if, in the opinion of the other passengers, he has managed to get within about five car lengths of the chosen object.

The game can be played as a competition, with all the passengers closing their eyes when the object is pointed out. In this version, the winner is the *last* person to call *before* the object is actually reached.

Round the Bend

On the open road, where there are long stretches without traffic, it is fun to try and guess when the next car will appear around the next bend ahead.

When a contestant thinks that a car is about due, he should call 'Honk-honk': the winner is the *last* person to call before a vehicle comes into sight.

Played this way, the competition is one of pure luck. Occasionally, however, one comes across stretches of road where a distant vehicle will disappear for a short while behind some hill, hedge, or dip in the road before re-emerging. In such cases some degree of skill and judgement is required in guessing when the car will reappear – and, if anything, this is somewhat more exciting than blind guessing on the next corner.

All Change

One way to avoid boredom in a car is to seek amusement even in irritating situations – a succession of traffic-light hold-ups, for instance.

On being halted by a red light, each occupant of the car should try to guess how long it will be before the light changes to amber.

When he thinks that the light is due to change, he should call 'Change!'

The winner is the last person to call before the amber light shows.

The fun lies in seeing how long one dares to delay before making a call. Too early a call means that someone else may get in a later bid – too long a delay, and the amber guillotine may chop off your chance of making any bid at all.

Number-plate games

Games and competitions based on the number-plates of parked or passing vehicles.

From A to Z

This is a family project rather than a competition, and is one of the most widely played of all number-plate games. The object is to spot the alphabet (in its proper order) on the number-plates of parked or passing vehicles.

As soon as an occupant of the car spots a number-plate containing the letter A (e.g. AGM or YFA) he or she calls out 'A'. Everyone then scans the road for a plate containing the letter B. When this has been found they search for C – and so on until the entire alphabet is complete.

As we have already said, the letters must be spotted in alphabetical order, which means that you cannot claim a K until all the letters up to and including J have been spotted.

If a plate bears not only the number being sought, but also the next letter (or letters) in the alphabet, the additional letter (or letters) may be claimed from that plate. For instance, if the alphabet has reached J, and a car should come along with the letters K M L, both the K and the L could be claimed.

Completing the whole alphabet in this way can sometimes take quite a long time, and it is not a bad idea to place a time limit (say half an hour) on the project. The aim then becomes to see how far one can get in that half hour. You can then repeat the game at some later stage in the journey to see if the team can get farther through the alphabet in half an hour than on the first attempt.

My Word

This game takes considerably less time than alphabet-spotting, and there is also an element of competition in it.

Each contestant chooses for himself some simple four-letter word such as 'beat' or 'tall', and jots it down on a piece of paper. He then scans the oncoming traffic for number-plates containing any of the letters of his word. Whenever such a letter is spotted, he should cross that letter out from his word. The order in which the letters are crossed out is unimportant, but only one letter may be claimed from any one number-plate.

ANTIDISESTABLISHMENTARIANISM
ANNUAL COACH TRIP

The first to complete the spelling of his word is, of course, the winner of that round.

If traffic is heavy, competitors should choose five- or six-letter words instead of four-letter ones.

Filling Up

The object of this competition is for passengers to make up words by taking the letters of a number-plate, and fitting other letters in between them.

The rule is that the first letter on the number-plate must be the initial letter of the word, and the last letter on the number-plate must be the final letter of the word. Any intervening letters must appear in their correct order somewhere in the middle of the word.

For example, the number-plate R B D could be made into the word 'rebound' by inserting the letter *e* between the *r* and *b*, and the letters *o u n* between the *b* and *d*, but you could not make up the word 'board' from R B D, because in board the *r*, *b*, and *d* do not appear in their correct order.

The first person to make up five words in this manner is the winner of the game.

36

An alternative version is for all the competitors to work on the same combination of letters chosen from some passing number-plate. In this case the winner is the one who manages to produce the *shortest* word in the space of one minute. In the case of RBD, the word 'rabid' would, for instance, beat either rebound or robbed, since rabid has only five letters.

Anagrams

The object of this game is for the contestants to spot number-plates bearing letters from which it is possible to make anagrams. For instance, the registration letters ODR may be shuffled around to form the word 'rod'. For each anagram composed in this way the player is awarded one point. Sometimes it is possible to make more than one anagram from a group of letters, and in this case each word formed counts as one point. Thus from the registration letters RMA, it is possible to form three words: arm, mar, and ram. For spotting this plate and announcing these anagrams, the player would score three points.

Occasionally one may come across a set of letters which already spell out a word, e.g. ACT. For spotting such a word on a number-plate the player scores three points straight away. If he is sharp enough to notice that not only do the letters form a word as they stand, but that they can also be formed into the anagram cat, he scores an extra point – making four points in all for that plate.

The first player to score a total of ten points wins the game.

Slogans

This competition provides an opportunity for those who pride themselves on their sense of humour to prove themselves. The idea is to take the letters of an oncoming number-plate, and to make up a slogan or

comment in which the words start with the same letters as those displayed on the plate – in their correct order. For example:

WFT   What's for tea?
SYL   See you later!
GR   Good riddance!
NSB   None so blind!

A variation of the game is to keep an eye out for plates the letters of which represent recognized abbreviations, such as:

COL   Colonel
FBI   Federal Bureau of Investigation
PTO   Please turn over

or the initials of famous people, such as:

WSC   Winston Spencer Churchill
MTT   Mao Tse-tung

38

One point can be awarded for each slogan, abbreviation, or set of initials spotted, though the real object is to see who can produce the wittiest or most ingenious efforts.

The Devil's Own

This game derives its name from the fact that it revolves about the number thirteen, which is often thought of as the devil's own number. Any number-plate the figures of which add up to more than thirteen is called an 'angel', and any number plate on which the figures add up to thirteen or less than thirteen is called an 'imp'. If a number-plate happens to have more than three digits only the last three of them count.

To begin with, someone is appointed 'referee'. If only two people are playing, then each acts as referee for his opponent. The referee's task is simply to point out an approaching car while it is still too far away for the number-plate to be read, and ask the player whose turn it is whether the plate is an angel or an imp. The player must reply promptly, and when the car passes the numbers on its plate are added up.

If the player's guess is right he is awarded one point, and is entitled to another turn. He continues as the guesser (scoring one point for each correct guess) until he gets one wrong. He does not lose any points for guessing wrongly, but the play then passes to the next contestant, who becomes guesser until he in turn makes a wrong guess.

The first person to score thirteen points is the winner.

A variation of this game is for the players to guess whether the numbers on the plate nominated by the referee add up to an odd or even total, in which case the player announces his guess by saying 'Odd' or 'Even' as soon as the approaching vehicle is pointed out. In this case it does not matter how many digits are displayed on the plate – they are all added together to arrive at the odd or even total. The winner is again the player who first scores a total of thirteen points.

As with most car games, handing matches to competitors is a better way of keeping the score than writing on paper.

Seven Up

This is a game which, apart from being fun, provides good practice in arithmetic. The aim is for competitors to keep their eyes skinned for passing number-plates, the digits of which can be shuffled around in one way or another to produce a total of seven.

Some plates will, of course, be quite easy. If, for instance, you spot the number 412 you can call 'Seven up! Four plus one plus two make seven!' Or in the case of 29 – 'Seven up! Two from nine leaves seven!'

The digits in a number may be taken in any order that one likes. For instance, in the case of 251, a player could claim 'Five from twelve leaves seven'.

If young children are playing it is best to limit the calculations to addition and subtraction, but older ones might like to try their hand at multiplication and division as well. For instance, in the case of 231, one could say 'Two threes are six and one makes seven' or even 'Twenty-one divided by three is seven.' But whatever mathematical tricks are used, *all* the numbers appearing on the plate *must* be utilized.

Score one point for each 'Seven up' combination spotted. The winner is the first person to get three clear points ahead of his closest rival.

Lucky Number

Each contestant chooses and announces a 'lucky number' – any number from 0 to 9. His task is then to spot this lucky number on the plates of parked or passing traffic.

He then scores one point for every time he spots his number, but if his lucky number appears *on a plate twice in succession*, he gets five points. If his number appears *on a plate three times in succession*, he gets ten points. For instance, if 5 is the number he is looking for, then:

A number like 459 would count as *one* point.

A number like 535 would count as *two* points.

A number like 554 or 955 would count as *five* points.

And the number 555 would count as *ten* points.

Scores are most easily kept by an umpire handing out matches, and the first person to acquire twenty matches wins the game.

Summing Up

In this version of number-spotting, each contestant should choose and announce a certain number, with the object of spotting a number-plate which adds up to his chosen number. A contestant can choose any number he likes, but he should opt for some number between 10 and 20, since the mathematical chances are greatest in this range.

On spotting a plate which adds up to his chosen total, the player should declare his find, score one point and announce a new number for his next search. Every time a claim is made, the other competitors are entitled to change their own number choices if they so wish.

The first player to score three points wins the game. *Summing Up* can be played as a team effort, in which case the aim is to spot *in order* number-plates which add up to every total from one to ten. In this hunt the main difficulty is usually getting a start, for number-plates totalling one are few and far between – 1, 10, and 100 being the only possibilities on plates which are limited to three digits. Plates totalling two are somewhat easier, because there are now six possibilities – 2, 11, 20, 101, 110, and 200, and the higher numbers become progressively easier.

The highest total possible with a three-digit number is, of course, twenty-seven (999), so one could try spotting plates summing up to every number from 1 to 27. But it is not advisable to try to spot these twenty-seven totals *in order* – it could take you all day. If you do want to spot the twenty-seven totals it is best to jot down a list of all the numbers from 1 to 27, and cross each one out as it is spotted. Even so, the chances are that you will have to pass about 1000 cars before your list is completely eliminated.

Treble Chance

Another version of number-spotting is to allow each player to choose and write down any three digits he likes. His object is then to spot number-plates made up exclusively of these three digits.

For instance, if one were to choose the digits 5, 7, 8, any of the following numbers (and quite a few others) would score a point: 5, 7, 8, 55, 57, 87, 577, 758, 888. But if the plate shows any digit which is not included

in one's treble-chance choice, that plate fails to score – 765 for instance would fail to score because it contains a 6, which was not one of the three numbers chosen.

The winner of the round is, of course, the person who first spots a plate made up exclusively of his chosen numbers.

Put and Take

This is an arithmetical game in which the aim is to achieve a total of ten. Each player is provided with a pencil and a scrap of paper on which to do his calculations, and someone is appointed 'caller'.

The job of the caller is to announce the *first* digit on the number-plates of oncoming vehicles. The first number to be called is written down by everyone. From then on, each player is free to decide for himself whether he will add or subtract the next number (and any subsequent numbers) to be called. For instance, imagine that the first five numbers to be called are

44

7, 6, 4, 8, 3. One player's calculations may look like this:

Add or subtract	Number called	Running total
	7	7
+	6	13
−	4	9
+	8	17
−	3	14

Meanwhile, on the same sequence of numbers, another player may choose to add or subtract in this way:

Add or subtract	Number called	Running total
	7	7
−	6	1
+	4	5
+	8	13
−	3	10

In this case the second player wins because he is the first to reach the total *ten*.

A player decides on whether to add or subtract a number only after he has heard the number called, and the caller should make sure that everyone has had a chance to make his current computation before spotting the next plate and making a further call.

Traffic Bingo

On a scrap of paper, each player sketches out nine squares arranged in this fashion (Fig. 1):

Fig. 1. Traffic Bingo

He then fills in the blank squares with nine numbers of his own choice – each number consisting of two digits.

One occupant of the car is then appointed 'caller'. It is his duty to call out the *last two* digits on the number-plate of each approaching car. In the event of a number-plate having only a single digit, that plate is ignored.

Any player who happens to have the called number on his or her card should cross it through.

The winner of the round is the first person to get three crosses in a line (either vertically, horizontally, or diagonally) and this should be announced by calling 'Bingo'.

Plate Pairing

A car-park or a beach promenade is probably as good a place as any for this competition in which the object is for people to scout around in search of cars bearing identical numbers.

One may think that the chances of spotting two identical numbers are fairly slim, but this is not so. Despite the 999 possibilities represented by one-, two-, or three-digit numbers, the mathematical chances are in favour of finding a pair of identical numbers in any group of thirty-eight or more vehicles.

The competition could, of course, be staged while travelling along the open road, the competitors trying to spot pairs of numbers on the plates of oncoming traffic. This, however, would involve jotting down all passing numbers in order to prove that one had really spotted a pair. The advantage of the car-park or promenade is that the competitor can be made to point out the matching pair which he claims to have spotted.

Clocking Along

Games and guessing competitions in which a clock, watch, or speedometer are used.

Milestones

'How far have we gone?' suddenly asks the driver — or anyone else in the car for that matter. And each occupant of the car is entitled to one guess.

The front-seat passenger adjudicates the guesses by reference to the milometer – a simple enough procedure

provided a note has been kept of the reading at the beginning of the journey, or if the car has a trip-meter which was set to zero when the trip commenced.

The winner is, of course, the person whose guess is closest to the milometer reading, and all contestants are honour-bound not to take a peek at the instrument before making their guesses.

The contest can be repeated at odd intervals during a long journey.

Five Minutes by Car

This competition can be staged in any sort of traffic conditions – indeed, sudden changes in traffic density can even add to the fun of the game.

The idea is to see how closely passengers can guess the distance that will be travelled in the next five minutes.

The front-seat passenger (as the one who can most easily keep an eye on both the milometer and the car clock) is in the best position to act as adjudicator. (If the car has no clock, then of course a watch may be used.)

As the clock's minute hand passes one of the five-minute marks, the adjudicator notes down the milometer reading, and calls for estimates of how far each person thinks the car will travel in the next five minutes.

When the clock's minute hand reaches its next five-minute mark, the adjudicator again consults the milometer, and works out how far the car has travelled, by comparing the new reading with the old one. The person whose guess is closest to the actual distance travelled during the five minutes is declared the winner.

Measured Mile

This competition is the converse of the previous one. The object here is not to guess how far one will travel in a certain time, but to estimate how long it will take to travel a certain distance – say one mile.

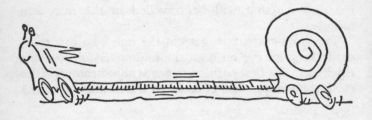

As the milometer ticks over to a new unit, the front-seat passenger calls 'Ready, steady, go!' Each passenger in the car then waits until he or she thinks the car has travelled exactly one mile, at which point the guesser calls 'Mile up!'

The winner is the *last* person to call 'Mile up!' *before* the milometer reaches a new unit.

When contestants become too proficient (as they soon do) at guessing a mile, the distance to be guessed may be extended to three or five miles. Judging these longer distances can be extremely tricky, especially if traffic conditions vary, as they do when leaving a built-up area for the open road or vice versa.

The umpire cannot himself compete in this contest because it is his duty to keep an eye on the milometer as it approaches the proper mark.

Mickles to the Mile

In this very simple game someone nominates a particular sort of roadside feature (such as a church, crossroad, farm gate, or telephone pole) likely to be encountered in the neighbourhood through which one is passing.

Each passenger then guesses how many of these designated objects will be passed in the course of the next five miles. The entire party assists in spotting the feature named, and in keeping count of how many are passed.

The distance is checked by referring to the milometer, and the person whose guess turns out to be closest to the actual number spotted becomes the winner of the round – and as such is entitled to nominate what feature should be spotted for the next five miles.

Rush-hour Check

This competition is most fun on fairly busy roads, the object being for competitors to guess how many vehicles one will meet in the course of the next minute.

A watch (preferably one which has a second hand) should be used by the adjudicator, whose task it is to announce the competition by asking 'How many

vehicles shall we meet in the course of the next minute –
counting from ... Now?' (timing the 'Now' to
coincide with the beginning of a new minute).

Each competitor should then announce promptly his
or her estimate. Meanwhile the adjudicator counts all
oncoming vehicles (including everything from bicycles
to steam-rollers, but excluding any parked vehicles).

The contestant whose guess proves to be closest to the
actual total is, of course, the winner.

Touring Teams

Games in which roadside objects are used to simulate popular sports and other activities.

'Local' Tennis

For a game of *'Local' Tennis*, each of two players chooses one side of the road as his 'court'.

Each time an inn or hotel is spotted by a player on his side of the road it counts as a winning rally. Thus the first player to spot a 'local' would call 'Fifteen-love'. A local spotted by his opponent would bring the score to 'Fifteen-all', and so on, the score being calculated as in ordinary tennis. (Just in case you may have forgotten, the progressive scores in tennis are 'love, fifteen, thirty, forty, game'.)

As in tennis, if both players happen to be on the 'forty' mark together, 'deuce' is called. The first player to score after deuce is said to have the 'advantage'. If that player again scores the next point, he wins 'game', but if his opponent scores, the score reverts to deuce. This continues until a point is scored by the player who, at the time, happens to have the advantage.

If, after a game has been won, the match is to continue, the players (as in real tennis) change courts for the next game, i.e. they swap sides.

Innings

This is a motoring version of French Cricket, and is called '*Innings*' because, like '*Local*' *Tennis*, it is based on inn signs.

It is played by two players who may toss a coin or a matchbox to decide who shall bat first.

The 'batsman' keeps an eye open (on both sides of the road) for inn signs depicting creatures with legs, and for every leg he spots he counts one run. Thus The White Hart would count as *four*, while The Green-man would count as *two*. The batsman continues adding runs to his score until his opponent spots an inn sign which has no legs at all, for instance The Crown and Sceptre. The batsman is then out, and it is his opponent's turn to have an innings.

It is not necessary for the legs themselves actually to

be painted on the sign. So long as the name *implies* a creature with legs it counts. Moreover, a plural name counts as *two* creatures. Thus The Hare and Hounds would score *twelve* – four legs for the hare, and eight for the (two) hounds. The only exception to this rule is when the inn sign actually specifies the number, e.g. The Five Geese undoubtedly represents ten legs.

A match consists of one innings each, the winner being the player who scored most runs (i.e. spotted most legs) during the course of his innings.

Ping-pong

This is an extremely simple game suitable for anyone old enough to count.

One player takes one side of the road as his 'court' while his opponent takes the other. Each player then merely counts aloud the number of cars *parked* on his side of the road. As in the real game of *ping-pong*, the first player to reach twenty-one wins that game.

If there is a third person who can act as umpire so much the better. It is his job to see that no parked vehicle is counted until the car you are in is actually abreast of it.

Only cars parked parallel to the road along which you are travelling count. Cars parked down side streets do not count even though they may be in sight.

Cricket Tour

Heavy or congested traffic is not suitable for this game which is best played on the open road where traffic density is only about one vehicle every quarter of a mile or so. The game is played between two people, and ideally there should be a third passenger to act as umpire.

The younger player bats first, the 'umpire' calling 'Play!' as soon as the car you are travelling in rounds the next corner.

The 'batsman' now has to keep his eye on all approaching cars with a view to scoring *one run* for each occupant (including the driver) of every oncoming car, except that:

(a) If the car is driven by a woman, the batsman scores a boundary, i.e. *four* runs (irrespective of how many occupants there are in the car);

(b) if the car is a two-seater sports model, the batsman scores a '*sixer*'.

The batsman continues adding to his score in this way until some vehicle which is not a private motor car in the usual sense of the term (e.g. a coach, bus, commercial truck, van, or motorbike) is spotted by his opponent, the 'fieldsman'. When he spots such a vehicle, the fieldsman should cry 'Howzat?' and the umpire then decides whether the appeal should be allowed. If he decides that the vehicle pointed out is *not* a private motor car, the umpire should declare the batsman 'bowled out'.

A batsman may also be given 'caught out' if (on an appeal by the fieldsman) the umpire decides that the batsman has miscounted the number of occupants in any car when claiming his runs.

Parked vehicles do not count, either for runs or dismissals.

After a batsman has been given 'out', it is his opponent's turn to bat, and the new innings begins when the umpire again calls 'Play!' as the car in which you are travelling reaches the next corner.

The game is ideal for two back-seat passengers as the players, with the front-seat passenger acting as umpire. If the umpire is ever uncertain about a decision, he should give the batsman the benefit of the doubt. Any player disputing the umpire's ruling automatically forfeits the match.

Bus Stop Billiards

In this game each bus stop spotted counts as a 'pot' and scores three points.

Each person standing at a bus stop counts as a 'canon' and scores two points – in addition to the three points scored for the bus stop itself.

The younger of the two players takes first 'break', and scores the appropriate number of points for each bus stop or would-be passenger he spots. He continues doing this until his opponent spots a bus itself coming from the opposite direction to that in which the players themselves are travelling. This entitles him to call 'Break!'

It is now the second player's turn to watch for bus stops and would-be passengers, scoring points for each one that is seen until his opponent spots an approaching bus and calls 'Break!'

The first player now resumes his watch for bus stops, adding any new scores to the total he reached during his previous break.

The game continues in this fashion until one player reaches twenty or some other previously agreed total, and he becomes the winner.

Soccer

This game is highly suitable for urban travel.

The pitch is any zebra-crossing. The goal-posts are the striped beacon-posts at either end of the crossing. And the footballers are the pedestrians.

The two opponents in the car are the team managers, and each takes one side of the road as his end of the field. Every time the car approaches or halts at a zebra crossing, the pedestrians crossing the road are watched.

The *last* person in possession of the 'pitch' (i.e. the last person to step off the crossing before your car crosses it) scores a goal for the side from which he *came*. Many a goal has been scored in this game by some young, athletic type making a quick last-minute dash, or by a dear old lady who is not quite sure which way she is going. If only one person is seen to cross, he or she of course scores a goal for the side from which he or she came.

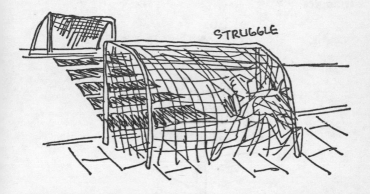

STRUGGLE

The first time the car passes a zebra-crossing on which no pedestrian has been spotted, is 'Half Time' and (as in real soccer) the teams 'change ends' (i.e. the team managers swap sides of the road).

The next time a car passes an unused zebra crossing, that is 'Full Time', and the team manager who has scored most goals in the two halves added together is the winner of the match.

Under no circumstances should team managers be tempted to lean out of the car and urge their sides on. You may be quite sure that any such barracking would be strongly resented by the 'players', who would be fully justified in calling a policeman and having you all detained as lunatics.

Road-sign Golf

There are two main kinds of traffic signs to be seen on the roads:

(a) Mandatory signs (e.g. 'No Entry', 'Lorries Prohibited', 'Speed Limit 30') which are enclosed in circles.

(b) Warning or hazard signs (e.g. 'Steep Hill', 'Hump Bridge', 'Double Bend') which are enclosed in triangles.

These are the only two types of sign used in *Road-sign Golf*. Signs of any other shape are ignored.

The circular (mandatory) signs represent the holes.

The triangular (hazard) signs represent the golfing hazards.

The contestants play each hole together, and each keeps the score of his *opponent*.

The players 'tee-up' as the car passes the first cross-road or side-road after the previous 'hole'.

When a hazard (triangular sign) is passed, the first player to name it correctly claims it as one stroke *against his opponent's score.* A wrong identification counts as *two* strokes against the *spotter* instead of one against his opponent. (The signs are usually illustrated and named in the back of motoring club handbooks, and in most road atlases, which should be consulted in any dispute over the proper meaning of a sign.)

The hole ends for *both* players when *either* of them spots and correctly identifies a mandatory sign (enclosed in a circle). The circular sign counts as *one* stroke against the score of the player who has spotted and named it, and also counts as *two* strokes against the score of his opponent.

A player who names a circular sign before his opponent has named a triangular one, can claim to have 'holed in one'.

The player with the smallest number of strokes against him wins that hole, and the players tee-up afresh for the next hole as soon as the car passes the next crossroad or side-road.

The winner is the player who wins most holes out of nine. Alternatively the number of strokes registered against each player for all nine holes can be totalled, and the player with the smallest total is the winner of the match.

A 'Stop' sign (which is enclosed in both a circle and a triangle) means that the hole being played must be abandoned on account of rain, and replayed – all strokes to date for that particular hole being cancelled.

Show Poker

Pencil and paper are essential for this game, which is suitable only for older children or adults.

One player is appointed 'dealer', and his duty is to call out the numbers of approaching vehicles, the digits of these numbers being 'dealt' out one at a time in rotation to the players. Each player jots down the digits he has been dealt until all players have five digits.

Each player now sorts his five digits into the best possible hand he can contrive, remembering that a 1 represents the Ace (the highest 'card' in the pack) and that a 0 is 'wild', i.e. it can be assigned any value that the player cares to give to it.

When all players have sorted their hands into order, they compare hands to discover who is the winner. The hands rank in this order (from highest to lowest):

Four-of-a-kind, i.e. four digits all the same with one odd card over, e.g. 88883 or 77702 (the 0 being nominated as a 7). Any player with 'five-of-a-kind' is disqualified for presumed cheating, even if he didn't cheat.

Full house, i.e. three digits of one value and a pair of another value, e.g. 33355 or 10044 (the two zeros being nominated as Aces). Between two 'full houses', the higher *trio* wins. For instance 77722 beats 66699.

Straight, i.e. five digits in numerical sequence, e.g. 45678 or 23406 (the 0 being nominated as the 5). Between two 'straights' the higher one wins. For instance 45678 beats 23456.

Odd or Even Flush, i.e. all five digits being odd, or all five being even, e.g. 13579 or 24466.

Three-of-a-kind, i.e. three digits of the same value, and two odd ones, e.g. 44496.

Two-pair, i.e. a pair of one value and a pair of another value, with one odd card, e.g. 22778.

One-pair, i.e. a pair of the same value and three odd cards, e.g. 55938.

High-card, i.e. where none of the above combinations occurs, the person holding the highest card wins. If this is a tie, the next card in value decides the winner, e.g. 97542 beats 96543, because while both tie with 9, the next card in the first hand, which is a 7, beats the 6 in the second hand.

Badminton

For this version of *Badminton*, the court is the road, the net is the dotted white line running along the centre, and the shuttlecock is a box of matches (or any other convenient small object).

One player takes the left of the road as his service court, and his opponent takes the other.

When a solid white line appears to the left or right of the dotted line, the shuttle (i.e. the matchbox) is claimed by the player serving from that side of the road.

If now a solid white line should appear on the opposite side of the road, the 'server' (i.e. the person holding the shuttle) passes the shuttle to his opponent.

As in real *Badminton*, only the server can win points. This means that the shuttle is passed back and forth between the players as described above *until* a solid white line appears on that side of the road representing the player who is *at that moment holding the shuttle*. That is 'game' to that player.

The players then change courts for the next game, *the winner of the previous game retaining the shuttle as server for the beginning of the next game.*

A match consists of three games, the 'champion' being the first player to win two of them.

(If a solid white line should later turn into a double white line, the shuttle is passed across as usual. But if both sides of a double white line begin simultaneously, that counts as a 'let', and the shuttle is retained by whoever is holding it.)

Take-over Bid

This game is an imitation of the game of big business rather than of sport.

To begin with, each of two players is given ten matches to represent his working capital.

One of the players now nominates one of the big oil companies (e.g. Shell) and makes a 'bid' (of one or more matches) to buy the next Shell service station they pass. He holds the matches representing the bid between his thumb and forefinger, retaining the rest of his capital in the other hand.

At the same time, the other player makes a bid (which may be larger, smaller, or the same as his opponent's bid) to buy the next service station belonging to some other large oil company (e.g. Esso).

A player wins his contract if he is the first to spot a service station for which he has bid. For this, he receives from his opponent the equivalent (in matches) of his own successful bid, *plus* the matches of his opponent's unsuccessful bid.

The loser of each 'contract' is entitled to have first bid (i.e. first choice of oil company) for the next round. He may either stick to his original company or change to another.

The winner of the game is the player who 'bankrupts' his opponent by winning from him his entire stock of matches.

Teach Them Young

Projects for older children who are beginning to take more interest in adult activities than in competitive games.

Census Count

Among those pastimes which, on a longish journey, can encourage an intelligent interest in the passing scene is *Census Count.*

The only equipment needed is an RAC or AA handbook which gives the population figures for each of the centres listed.

On passing through any town or village listed in the handbook, the 'Chief Census Officer' should invite everyone (including himself) to guess the population of the place.

Guesses should be announced as the car emerges from the built-up area, and should be adjudicated by the census officer using the handbook as his source of reference.

Traffic Cop

For anyone who is beginning to be interested in driving procedure and the rules of the road, an instructive pastime is to spend half an hour or so (preferably in the front seat) making a critical appraisal of other road users. The 'traffic cop' should jot down brief notes describing any instances of excessive speed, crossing of double white lines, bad signalling, dangerous over-taking, and any other faults he notices among drivers on the road.

It is an excellent way to teach children the art of road observation, which will stand them in good stead when the time comes for them to take the wheel. It also helps to make them very aware of the dangers of careless driving and law-breaking. It might even help to keep you on your toes – unless of course you are prepared to suffer the indignity of being 'booked'.

Navigator

Nearly all children enjoy acting as navigator when travelling through unfamiliar roads on a longish journey.

The 'navigator' needs either a road-map or a road-atlas, and should be told both the route to be taken and the destination. His first task is to identify accurately the car's position on the map, and examine the route ahead with a view to keeping the driver informed as to what lies ahead. He should also keep an eye on signposts, traffic signs, filter lanes, and any other features which may affect the driver's course of action.

The navigator can help the driver by navigational comments such as: 'This is the village of Littleton ... Signposts coming up ... We still have six miles to

Bigville ... Should be crossing the B111 any time now ... Roundabout ahead ... We need the right-hand lane ... Take the third exit ... We turn right half a mile past the railway bridge.'

The navigator must make his comments brief and to the point – neither overdetailed, nor overfrequent – and give the sort of information that the driver asks for. Above all, he must remember that the driver, and the driver alone, is responsible for the control of the vehicle.

Navigating is so excellent an introduction to roadcraft that everyone should be encouraged to do it whenever a longish journey is being undertaken.

Log Book

In this technological age there are many tasks that call for the precise recording of data. Keeping a 'log book' is an easy way to develop the technique!

Any cheap exercise book will do, the pages of which should be ruled into columns (two narrow and one wide) so that entries can be tabulated in this fashion:

Date and time	Speedo reading	Details
3 July		
10·05	23865	Richley. 8 gals 4-star. 1 pt oil. Checked tyres. Off-side front 4 lbs low. Faulty valve replaced.
10·10	23867	Heavy rain.
10·25	23871	Passed through Ombord. Traffic congested.
10·40	23881	Reached Awling. Average speed from Ombord 40 mph.

If one is particularly interested in petrol consumption, a separate column can be ruled in to record purchases.

This book can be kept in the gloves-compartment, and made up regularly throughout the journey as things happen.

Parents should try to take an interest in the project. Occasionally during the course of the journey suggest an entry, and read over the entries attentively at the end of the day. Everyone likes to feel that he has done something worthwhile and deserving of attention – and keeping a log book *is* a worthwhile project.

Holiday Journal

Holiday Journal is for those who are more interested in literary and artistic pursuits than in keeping a log book.

The idea is to compile an interesting and informative record of a journey or holiday.

Ideally you need both a small notebook and an exercise book. The notebook is used for jotting down brief details while travelling, which may then be written up in proper narrative style either during roadside breaks or in the evening.

The traditional way of keeping a journal is to write up each day's events in the order in which they occur with entries like: '*Jane's hat blew into the sea while she was trying to photograph the seagulls.*' Personal anecdotes of this sort can raise many a laugh when you come to read over them after the holiday, but they are usually of interest only to those who were there on the occasion, and whose own memories fill in the details. Other people are more likely to be interested in a book dealing with individual sights, and written in the style of a guide book rather than a personal day-to-day journal. In such a book the entries should be under subheadings, with the date of one's visit in brackets at the end, e.g.:

GUNWALLOE CHURCH. *Fourteenth-century church built so close to the sea that spray from the sea sometimes dashes over it. The tower is not joined to the church itself, but is about 15 feet away, and built right into the cliff face. The remains of a prehistoric fortress can be seen nearby.* (1.8.76)

The book can be embellished with postcards bought locally, tourist leaflets, theatre programmes, or anything else that will help to bring the story to life.

One advantage of keeping a journal in this guide book form is that you can become something of an authority on the places described, and if, some time later, a friend or acquaintance intends visiting the area, you can suggest to them the sights that are worth seeing.

Tourist Courier

If you are planning a long car trip, why not ask one of the older children to act as 'courier' for the journey?

A day or so before you set out, explain to the courier where you are going and the route you propose to take. Provide him with a map and some reference material such as a guide book for the area. (Excellent guide books, such as the *Ward Lock's Red Guide* series, are obtainable at a modest price from most bookshops.)

The courier can then read up details of any interesting places which you may be passing *en route*, making brief notes to help his commentary (and perhaps noting the relevant pages so that he can find them easily during the journey).

As you approach a town or other place of note, the courier can then tell the other passengers in the car any interesting details connected with it – that the town is the birthplace of a famous explorer, or that a battle was fought near by, or that the town square contains some fine specimens of Tudor architecture.

You can make the same arrangement when planning a day's excursion on holiday. Let the family courier study the guide book for the area, and suggest a route for the day's outing, visiting places of special interest, and giving a short chat on each place visited.

Service Manager

Young people approaching the age when they will be eligible for a driving licence can be made responsible for checking over the car, before setting out on an excursion.

You can give them a checklist of things to do, which could be something like this:

(a) Check that the handbrake is on and that the car is out of gear – a standard precaution before any other check is made on a vehicle.

(b) Check petrol gauge (for which the ignition key must be turned without starting the engine).

(c) Check oil level (using a tissue or old rag to wipe the dipstick).

(d) Check brake-fluid reservoir (to ensure that it is *right up to the mark*).

(e) Check radiator water level when engine is cold.

(f) Check water level in windscreen washer reservoir.

(g) Check that windscreen wipers work, and that their blades are free from grime (they can be wiped with a clean tissue).

(h) Check all lights – main-beam, dip, parking, tail, brake, and reversing lights. Trafficator lights, and dashboard indicators (such as generator and oil-warning lights) should be checked also.

(i) Inspect tyre treads, and remove any wedged stones, nails, or chips of glass.

(j) Check tyre pressures, being careful not to let out too much air in the process.

See You Later

On long journeys, children need an opportunity to stretch their legs, and a lunch-time or mid-afternoon break provides a good opportunity. If your passengers are old enough and responsible enough, let them set off along the road some ten minutes or so before you intend to resume the journey.

Explain the route you propose taking, so that they can hitch a lift from you when you catch up with them. Ten to twelve minutes' start is usually enough – you will probably be surprised to find how much distance a brisk walker can cover by the time you have caught up with him.

Keep an eye on the milometer, so that when you pick the children up you can tell them how far they have managed to hoof it.

On holiday, suggest to the older children that they might enjoy setting off on a cross-country hike to some village perhaps two or three miles away with a view to rendezvousing with the car at some specified time. Be quite specific about the route they are to take, the time of the rendezvous, and the exact location of the meeting-place – e.g. outside the village church, or 'at the shop where we bought the eggs last Saturday'.

PART TWO:
BACK SEAT PASTIMES

Games and pastimes which are suitable for whiling away the time during a tedious journey, but which could also be played during roadside stops, or in a tent, caravan, or guest-house on wet afternoons.

Handy Games

The following is a selection of simple games requiring little equipment other than one's own hands.

Follow My Finger

Each of the two players places his right hand behind his back, and manoeuvres his fingers into an unusual shape, e.g. the fist clenched, but with the thumb protruding between his middle fingers, or the thumb touching the ring-finger with the forefinger touching the little finger.

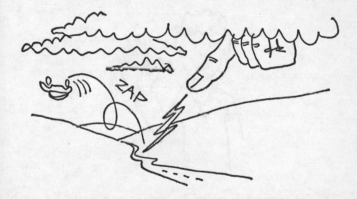

When both are ready they both show their hands on the order 'Show!' Each must then try to copy with his left hand the configuration shown by his opponent's right hand.

The winner of the round is the one who first manages

to reproduce the finger configuration shown by his opponent.

If, in the course of his manipulations, a player should let his own right-hand positioning slip, he forfeits the round.

Odds and Evens

In this game, one of the two players places his right hand either in his lap or across the front of his waist, and covers it with his left hand. Under cover of his left hand he then tucks under (if he so wishes) one or more fingers of his right hand, leaving the others extended.

His opponent then has to guess whether an odd or an even number of fingers have been left extended. (The thumb does not count.)

If the guesser is right, he scores one point for each extended finger: if he is wrong, his opponent scores one point for each extended finger.

The loser of each round becomes the finger-poser for the next round, and the winner becomes the guesser. The first player to score eleven points is the winner.

Tip the Scales

Two contestants are each supplied with six matches (or, if matches are unavailable, with six dried peas or other small objects).

One of the players now secretly distributes his stock of matches between his two hands in any manner he likes. For instance, he could put two in his left hand and four in his right, or all six in one hand with none in the other.

He then holds out his two clenched fists to represent a pair of scales, and his opponent is required to guess which way the 'scales' will 'tip', i.e. which hand is 'heavy' (holding more matches) and which is 'light' (with fewer matches) – or whether the scales are in fact 'balanced' (with an equal number of matches in each). Note that a player is required to distribute his *entire stock* of matches between his two hands, and not try to conceal any elsewhere about his person.

When the guess had been made, the first player must open his hands to show whether or not the guesser is right. If the guesser *is* right, the first player must hand over one match which is then added to his opponent's stock: if he is wrong, he must hand over one of his own matches.

The player who wins the round is the one who must act as Scales for the next round.

The game ends when one player finishes up with all twelve matches.

Heads and Tails

Any coin from a halfpenny to a fifty-pence piece will do for this back-seat version of *Pitch and Toss*.

One player conceals the coin between the palms of his hands which he then extends horizontally in front of him. His opponent has to guess whether a head or a tail is uppermost. After the guess has been announced, the first player must remove his top hand to reveal the coin. If the guess is right, the first player must again

conceal the coin, and the performance is repeated. If, however, the guesser proves to be wrong, it is he who must conceal the coin and leave it up to his opponent to do the guessing.

The winner is the first person to guess three right in a row.

Legs Eleven

All you need for this game are eleven matches and the tray of a matchbox in which to hold them.

Two players now take it in turns to claim either one, two, or three matches at a time from the store of matches in the box. Notice that a player *must* claim at least one match at each turn, but must not claim more than three.

The object of the game is not to see who finishes up with most matches, but which of the players finishes up with an *even* number of matches. Since there are eleven matches to begin with, one of the players must finish up with an even number of matches, and the other with an odd number. The player who finishes with an *even* number is the winner of the round.

The game is not so childish as you may be tempted to think. If you are determined to win, it calls for quite careful thought and calculation towards the end.

Car, Bridge, and River

This simple game requires no equipment other than one's hands. Each of the two players conceals his right hand under his left armpit, and prepares to adopt one of the three hand positions shown here (Fig. 2):

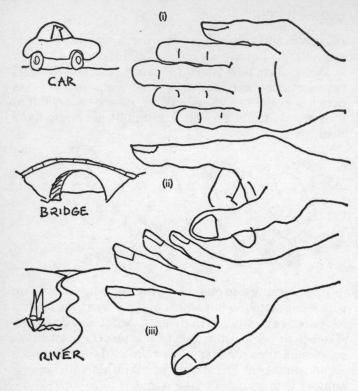

Fig. 2. Car, Bridge, and River

The hand held vertically (i) represents a *car* speeding along.
An extended forefinger (ii) represents a *bridge* spanning a river.
The hand spread horizontally (iii) represents the ripples of a river.

The players now take it in turns to call 'Show!', though this is a task which can be assigned to an umpire if there is a third person present.

Now:

(a) If one person shows a *car*, and the other shows a *bridge*, the car wins — *because a car can go over a bridge*.

(b) If one shows a *bridge*, and the other shows a *river*, the bridge wins — *because a bridge can go over a river*.

(c) If one shows a *river*, and the other shows a *car*, the river wins — *because a river can submerge a car* (when there is no bridge present).

Each of the three hand positions can either beat or be beaten by one of the other two positions, and a player scores one point for each win. Occasionally both players may show the same hand position, in which case that round is a draw.

It is most important that players show their hands immediately the word 'Show!' is called. Any hesitation or attempt to change the hand position after glimpsing the opponent's choice disqualifies that player and loses him the round.

The winner is the first person to achieve a total of five points.

Finger Mimes

Any number of players can take part in this game, the contestants taking it in turns to do the miming.

The mimer privately thinks of some word (preferably of about five or six letters) and then indicates each of the letters, in proper sequence, by hand-mimes.

Vowels are indicated by holding up one or more fingers according to the rule:

> One finger means A
> Two fingers mean E
> Three fingers mean I
> Four fingers mean O
> Five fingers mean U

Consonants are indicated by miming something the name of which begins with the letter being thought of.

For instance, to indicate the word 'shop', the mimer could firstly **s**nap his fingers to indicate *s*, secondly lay his hand on his **h**eart to indicate *h*, thirdly hold up four fingers to indicate *o*, and finally write with an imaginary **p**encil to indicate *p*.

The first person to guess the word being mimed is, of course, the winner of the round.

Balancing Act

The movement of the car can itself provide the basis for this simple competition, which has the added value of helping to accustom children to the environment of a moving vehicle.

The contestants are each provided with an identical small object (such as a matchbox, coin, or ball of crumpled paper).

They then take it in turns to issue challenges. The challenger prescribes the manner in which the object is to be balanced – for instance, on two outstretched fingers, on the left knee, or on the head – and both the challenger and the challenged now pose the object in the stipulated manner.

The first to let his object fall is the loser. If the challenger wins he scores one point, but if the challenged party wins, he scores two points. The first person to reach a total of six points is the winner.

Any challenge which would involve risk should be strictly forbidden.

At a Guess

Hot and Cold

At home, the game of *Hot and Cold* (or *Hunt the Thimble* as it is sometimes called) is played by someone roaming about the room in search of an object, the location of which is known to the other players, but not to the

searcher. He is guided by being told that he is getting warmer as he approaches the object, and colder as he moves away from it – closeness being indicated by words like 'Warm', 'Hot', 'Very hot', 'Scorching', and distance by words like 'Cool', 'Cold', 'Very cold', 'Freezing'.

In a car it is not practicable for the searcher to move about, but the game can be played by the searcher *naming* objects in the car, and being told (in terms of 'Hot' or 'Cold') whether his guess is close to or far away from some object secretly decided upon by the others. For instance, if the object sought is the windscreen wiper, and the searcher says 'Back window', he is obviously 'Very cold' if not 'Freezing'. If he next says 'Driver', this is 'Much warmer'. If he guesses 'Windscreen', he is of course 'Very hot'.

When the object has been identified, the turn of searcher passes on to another player until all the competitors have had a chance to identify some object.

What's My Line?

In this back-seat version of the famous television panel game, one of the occupants of the car imagines himself as belonging to one of the trades or professions, and announces 'I have just found a job'.

The other participants, representing the 'panel', then ask him leading questions which can be answered by a single word or simple phrase such as 'Yes', 'No', 'Sometimes', or 'I really don't know.'

The panel would be well advised not to guess haphazardly at different occupations, but to limit progressively the scope of their search by asking general questions such as: 'Are you self-employed?', 'Do you work inside or outside?', 'Do you work mainly with your hands?', and so forth.

If, after twenty or thirty questions, the panel has not guessed the trade or profession, the 'workman' wins, and should then declare his occupation. It then becomes someone else's turn to challenge the panel.

When the game is being played during the course of a journey, it may add to the interest by limiting the game to trades or professions which have something to do with travel, e.g. 'the man who paints the white lines on the road' or 'a baggage attendant at an airport'.

Who Am I?

This is another panel game, similar to *What's My Line?*, the main difference being that the challenger imagines himself as some famous character, either contemporary, historical, or fictitious, e.g. The President of the United States, the Queen of Sheba, or Little Bo-peep.

As with the previous game, the panel should gradually limit the field of their search by generalized questions, such as: 'Are you alive or dead?', 'Are you real or fictitious?'

The choice of character should take into account the age and scope of knowledge of the youngest member of

the panel. The game can also be made more fun by
including an occasional trick choice such as 'I am me',
or even 'I am you'.

Lip-reading

Lip-reading is an entertaining way of providing five or
ten minutes' diversion, especially for younger children.

One person silently mouths a proverb, a well-known
line of poetry, or anything else for that matter, while the

CRUSH

other (or others) tries to identify the words. If more
than one person is doing the guessing, the first to guess
the words correctly becomes the next one to do the
mouthing.

No Speak English

Imagine that you are on a continental tour, and that the
car has crossed the frontier into a country where none
of the inhabitants seems able to understand English.
Everyone is hungry, so you appoint someone to visit a
shop in search of food. The 'shopper' must decide
privately what it is that he or she wants to buy, and
must then perform a mime suggesting the item sought.

The rest of the players act as foreign shop assistants, and try to guess which food is being ordered. The first to guess it correctly becomes the shopper for the next round.

Lucky Dip

The baffling assortment of odds and ends usually to be found in a handbag forms the basis of this guessing competition. The only other thing required is a handkerchief, and the handbag may even be able to provide this as well.

The owner of the bag extracts from it some small item around which the handkerchief is wrapped. The bundled article is then passed to the competitors, who must try to identify it by feeling its outlines through the cloth.

Items like vanity cases, cigarette lighters, or purses can be identified fairly easily. Coins are somewhat more difficult if one insists on the guesser naming the actual denomination. Soft items, like a pound note, a bus ticket, or another handkerchief within the handkerchief can also be quite challenging.

Pig in a Poke

In this competition one of the players, acting as challenger, secretly inserts a small number of coins (not more than three or four) into an otherwise empty matchbox.

The matchbox is then handed to the other competitors who, by the weight of the box or the sound it makes when rattled, must try to guess how much the matchbox is worth.

The person whose guess is closest to the mark becomes the challenger for the next round. If two or more tie in their estimates, the original challenger refills the box with other (or perhaps even the same) coins, and presents it again for estimates.

Word Games

Games and contests based on manipulating words and letters.

Bear Baiting

One of the players is chosen as the bear to be baited. His role is to see how long he can continue to answer questions without using either of the words 'Yes' or 'No'.

The other players (the baiters) now fire questions at him as quickly as possible, phrasing the questions in such a way that the 'bear' may be tempted into using the forbidden words. For instance, if one of the baiters were to ask 'Has a horse got five legs?' the bear may avoid the use of 'No' by replying 'Not that I am aware of.' However, the question 'How many horses have five legs?' could very well evoke the response 'No horse has five legs.' The bear would then be out for having used the forbidden word 'No' in his reply.

In this game it is usually agreed that not only must the bear refrain from using the word 'No', but that he must also avoid saying 'know'. The game may be made still more difficult by also banning the old word 'Aye' which means 'Yes' – for this also rules out two other common words which are pronounced the same way – 'eye' and 'I'.

The baiter who poses the question which ultimately catches out the bear becomes the bear for the next round.

Belling Spee

An ordinary *Spelling Bee* has two main drawbacks as a pastime: it savours rather too much of schoolwork, and sometimes leads to arguments which can really be settled only by referring to a dictionary. So, for a change, and for a laugh, why not try a *Belling Spee*, in which people have to spell each word backwards?

The idea is to choose words which one's opponent could probably spell properly the right way around, but which are particularly difficult to spell backwards: 'church' is a good example of a short word in which most people get the *r* in the wrong place when trying to spell 'hcruhc'.

To begin with, each contestant is challenged to spell

a three-letter word backwards. If he makes a mistake he is out. However, if he goes back and corrects himself immediately it is treated as a let, and he is given one more chance on another three-letter word. A mistake on this, or again a self-correction, means that this time he must drop out.

Those who succeed with their three-letter words go on to the next round of four-letter words, then on to five-letter words – and so on until only one person remains in the contest – and he of course is the winner.

The job of choosing words to be spelled should be passed around to everyone in turn.

To check the backward spelling the safest course is for the person who chooses the word to select it from a newspaper, book, or magazine. With the printed word before him each letter can be checked as it is spoken.

Place Chain

This quite simple game commences with one player naming some city or town. The next player must then name another city or town beginning with the last letter of the previous place named, e.g.: Brighton ... Newport ... Torrington ... Norwich ...

There is no harm in letting contestants scan a road-atlas in their search, so long as they do not consult the

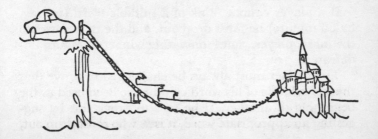

index, but a time limit (of, say, one minute) should be imposed on each turn. If a player fails to produce a name beginning with the appropriate letter before the minute has elapsed, he or she drops out. The last player remaining in the contest is the winner.

Silly-billies

The idea here is much the same as in *Place Chain*, except that the contestants are not confined to place-names, and it is the last *syllable* (instead of the last letter) that makes the chain.

One player begins the game by saying any word containing two or more syllables that he cares to choose. The next player must then think of a word *beginning* with the same syllable as the previous word *ended* with.

The last syllable of the second word then becomes the syllable with which the third player must begin his word – and so on.

If a player cannot think of a suitable word (in, say, half a minute) he must drop out, and the turn passes to the next player, until only the winner remains undefeated.

The winner must always be challenged to prove that the last syllable of his word could have been used as the beginning of another. If he fails to prove this by suggesting an appropriate word, it is *he* who must drop out, and those players who were defeated by his syllable regain their positions – commencing with the syllable which was used unfairly. For instance, the game could proceed thus:

carpet . . . petal . . . allow . . .

If no one can then think of a polysyllabic word beginning with *ow* (or *low*) the last person wins – provided he can prove that *he* could have thought of such a word, e.g. 'owlish'. If he cannot produce such a word, then it is he who must drop out, and the next player takes up the *al* (or 'petal') to form a word like 'algebra', and the game continues – perhaps with 'braggart'. (Notice that the common syllable – in this case *bra* – need not rhyme in the two words so long as it is spelt the same way.)

Oh! Oh!

This is a competition in which the players have to concentrate and keep their wits about them if they want to win.

One of the party reads aloud a paragraph from some book, newspaper, or other piece of print which happens to be available, while the other players try to spot all the letters *o* in the piece being read.

Whenever a player hears a word which contains an *o* he should cry 'Oh!' and the reading stops to see whether or not he is right. If he is right he scores one point. If he is wrong, he takes two points off whatever score he has at that time. The person with the highest score at the end of the paragraph is the winner of the round.

The extract should be read clearly and distinctly at

normal reading pace, i.e. about the speed used by radio news announcers. It should not be gabbled in an attempt to outpace the players.

The letter *o* is easily spotted in words like 'hot' and 'cough', but can easily be missed in words such as 'room', 'come', 'shout', and 'women', where it has a somewhat different sound.

Missing Vowels

A surprisingly challenging contest is for someone to think of a word, and then to spell it omitting all the vowels. The other members of the party must then try to insert vowels into the spelling to make a proper English word.

The word need not necessarily be the same word that the speller has thought of, so long as it contains the consonants in the order in which they were given. Thus, if the speller thought of the word 'rag' he would give it as 'rg', and 'rig', 'rug', 'rage', or 'rouge' would all be equally acceptable as answers. It is, however, necessary for the speller to have *some* word in his mind, since, if everyone fails, he may be challenged to prove that such a word does exist.

If it is your turn to spell, don't be tempted into thinking that the longer the word the more difficult it will be for the guessers. Fairly short words with lots of vowels – like 'enough' – are remarkably difficult to work with when spelled simply as 'ngh'. Notice, too, that in this case the word 'night' cannot be accepted as a legitimate answer because it contains the extra consonant *t*. Only vowels may be added to the consonants provided by the speller.

Alphabetics

The object of this pastime is to make up a grammatically correct (even if nonsensical) sentence which contains all the letters of the alphabet in their correct order. For example:

A backward Englishman from Brighton injured

and killed many hopeful squires through overwork, and executed a fly buzzing.

See who can complete the assignment in the fewest possible words – or even the fewest possible letters. But it is just as much fun to treat it as a family effort, each person contributing suggestions towards the brevity of the sentence!

Proverbial Fun

There are various ways in which proverbs can be used to provide ten or fifteen minutes' amusement. Here are four suggestions:

Initial Proverbs Someone thinks of a fairly short proverb, and gives the initial letters of each of its words in proper sequence, e.g. *i, t, t, t, m, a, q.* The other members of the party then try to identify the proverb – which in this case is 'It takes two to make a quarrel.'

In Other Words Proverbs are not of course meant to be taken literally. When we say 'A stitch in time saves nine' we are not really referring to sewing at all. The meaning of the proverb is that by giving immediate attention to small problems we may save ourselves much greater efforts later on when the problems may have grown bigger. Quite a lot of fun may be had by one person thinking of a proverb, and then paraphrasing it to describe its true meaning, whereupon the other members of the party try to guess the original proverb. For instance, if the proverbialist gives 'People who keep roaming about never acquire any property,' the other members of the party have to guess 'Rolling stones gather no moss.'

Proverbial Questions In this game, one member of the party thinks of some proverb, and then poses a question by which the proverb may be identified. For instance:

'What comes to those who wait?'

To which the answer is:

'All things come to those who wait.'

The contest may be made more difficult by posing the question in a paraphrased fashion instead of using the exact words of the proverb. For instance, one could ask:

'What should not be subjected to an oral examination?'

To which the answer is:

'A gift horse, for one should not look a gift horse in the mouth.'

Split Proverbs In this rather amusing pastime, two persons each privately decide upon some proverb. One of them then announces the first *half* of his proverb, and the other adds to this the second half of his own proverb. By allowing just a little freedom in the use of conjunctions and prepositions, the result can sometimes be quite amusing, as in the case of:

'Too many cooks in one basket', or 'the early bird catches a friend indeed'.

The players can then try swapping the unused halves of their proverbs to produce further inanities such as:

'Don't put all your eggs in to spoil the broth,' or 'A friend in need is the worm.'

Road-map Games

Games for which a road-map or road-atlas may be used.

My Aunt Flora

This is an excellent way to familiarize children with map study. In the search for *My Aunt Flora*, one of the players consults the road-map or road-atlas, and privately decides upon some town or village as the abode of his mythical Aunt Flora. Having made his decision, he then announces 'I am sure my Aunt Flora lives somewhere here, but where can it be?'

The other player (or players) then guesses by pointing to any town or village on the map.

In the almost certain event of the first guess being wrong, Aunt Flora's 'relative' should say, 'Not there I fear.'

The seeker then makes another guess, to which Aunt Flora's relative should respond, either by saying 'I think we are getting nearer,' or 'I think we are going the wrong way' (according to whether the second guess is nearer the mark or farther away from it than the first).

With each successive guess, the relative should indicate whether the guess is closer or farther away than the guess preceding it, until finally the seeker hits upon the right location.

Four Quarters

This too is a map searching game. One of the two players decides upon some feature appearing on the map, and announces whether it is a town, level crossing, inn, or whatever else it happens to be.

The other player then indicates one of the longitudinal (vertical) lines which invariably appear on a map, and asks whether the feature sought lies east or west of that line. On receiving the answer, he then indicates one of the latitudinal (horizontal) lines, and asks whether it is north or south of that line. This narrows his search to one quarter of the map, and he repeats this quartering process until he has located the square in which the feature lies. He can then narrow the search still further if necessary by laying a pencil or matchstick vertically or horizontally on that square and asking on which side of the pencil or matchstick the feature lies.

The object is to identify the feature sought in the fewest such quarterings.

Place Spotting

For this contest a road-map or road-atlas can conveniently be shared by two or even three people seated together. The map should be opened so that it shows the area through which the car is passing at the time.

One passenger then keeps an eye out for a roadsign, and announces the place-name and the distance shown on it. The contestants then try to locate that place on the map, the winner being, of course, the first to do so.

This is excellent practice at map reading, especially when the car happens to be travelling south, for places to the left of the road will then appear to the right of the road on the map, which means that the spotter has to keep his wits about him.

Lost Town

This extremely simple game is far more challenging than may appear at first sight.

From the index of a road-atlas or motoring guide, the 'adjudicator' reads out, slowly and distinctly, a list of five or six place-names. The competitors are then given a few seconds to chew the names over and try to fix them in their memory.

The adjudicator then reads out the list again – but in a different order, and omitting one of the names.

The winner of the round is the first person to announce the missing name correctly, and he becomes adjudicator for the next round.

Longish names which are veritable tongue-twisters should be avoided, since the object is to test one's memory, not one's pronunciation. If competitors become too skilled at recalling names, the list can be extended to six or even eight names, when recalling the missing one can prove quite difficult.

County Quiz

This is a very simply organized quiz which can teach one quite a lot about one's own country.

One member of the party takes a road-map or road-atlas and, consulting it for reference, poses questions such as:

(a) In which county is the town of Banbury?

(b) What is the number of the main road from London to Bath?

(c) How many other counties touch the county of Stafford?

Questions of this type are quite difficult enough for the average car passenger, and the question-master

should remember that a quiz in which no one can answer any questions at all is not much fun.

Each member of the party should be allowed to pose three questions before passing the map on to another person to act as question-master for the next three-question round.

Pencil and Paper

Pastimes involving the use of pencil and paper which are equally suitable for playing in the back seat of a car either while travelling or during a roadside halt. When the car is in motion, games involving writing should be kept short. It is better to use a felt-tipped pen or crayon rather than a pencil. In particular, whenever drawing is required, a crayon is far more satisfactory.

Lions and Christians

The game of *Noughts and Crosses* is too well known to need description, but here is a variation which may prove entertaining.

Four lines are drawn as for *Noughts and Crosses*, and the two opponents take it in turns to insert O's (representing the mouths of the lions) and +'s (representing the Christians) in the squares. The object however is not to get three O's or three +'s in a line, but to *avoid* getting three of a kind in a line (either horizontally, vertically, or diagonally). The player who forces his opponent to put a third O or + in a line is the winner.

The winner of each round has the task of opening the play for the next round (because, quite honestly, the first player is at a disadvantage).

Fields and Fences (or Squares)

Sixteen dots are placed in a square array as shown in Fig. 3. The two players now take it in turns to join pairs

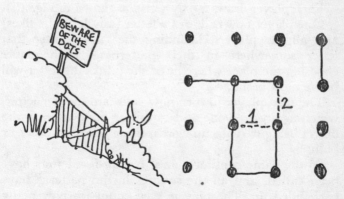

Fig. 3. Fields and Fences

of adjacent dots with a line (either vertically or horizontally). Whenever a player draws a line that completes a square he is entitled to claim that field by putting his initials in it. On completing a square he is also entitled to another turn.

If the game has reached the stage shown in Fig. 3, for instance, the next player could claim the bottom field by drawing in line 1, then draw in line 2 to give himself possession of the middle field, and still have one turn left to draw in a third line wherever he should choose.

The winner is the person who owns most of the nine possible fields when all the squares have been claimed.

Cross-words

You don't have to be a crossword solver in order to play this game. The idea is for you to make up your own 'cross-words' as you go along.

Each player draws a 5 by 5 grid as shown in Fig. 4(i).

One player now calls out a letter (any letter he likes) and all the players, including the caller, enter that letter somewhere in their patterns – each player choosing the place where he or she thinks the letter will prove most useful.

The next player in turn now calls out another letter, which again everyone adds to his or her pattern – the object being to make up words, either across or down or both.

So the game continues until twenty-five letters have been called, and all the squares in the patterns have been filled up. The players now count up how many English words they have managed to work into their patterns. Proper nouns like 'Tim' or 'Rome' do not count, neither do single letter words like 'A' or 'I'.

One point is scored for each letter of each word, either across or down. Thus, the example shown in

(i)

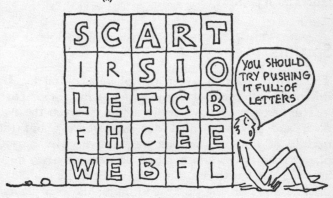

Fig. 4. Cross-words

Fig. 4(ii) (where the letters that count are shown in heavy print) would score as follows:

Across words	Score	Down words	Score
SCAR	4	HE	2
CAR	3	AS	2
CART	4	RICE	4
ART	3	ICE	3
LET	3	TO	2
WEB	3	BE	2

making a total of thirty-five points for the whole pattern.

Letters count more than once if they come into more than one word. The top line in this example for instance contains no fewer than four words: scar, car, cart, and art. It is surprising how many words some people can manage to work into a pattern in this way.

The winner is, of course, the person whose pattern scores most points.

Sprouts

This battle of wits between two players commences by drawing two large dots on the paper an inch or so apart.

The first player now draws a line between the two dots, and places a third dot somewhere about the middle of the line he has just drawn. The second player then draws another line between any two dots, and places a fourth dot somewhere about the middle of his new line. So the game continues, the two players taking it in turns to join any two available dots with a line, and placing a new dot in the middle of the newly-drawn line – subject to these rules:

(a) No line must cross another line.

(b) When a dot has three lines leading away from it, a ring is to be drawn around the dot to show that it is 'dead', and cannot be used again.

The player who cannot draw a line from one available dot to another without crossing an existing line loses the game.

In some cases, the game may finish up with only one unringed dot left. In this case, the player who placed that final dot is the winner, since it is impossible for his opponent to join it to any other.

The diagrams (Fig. 5) overleaf illustrate the way in which a game may develop.

In (i), the first player joins the two original dots (A and B) and places a third dot at C.

In (ii), his opponent joins A and C (going around B) and places a new dot at D. Since C now has three lines leading away from it, it is ringed to show that it is no longer available.

The first player then joins A and D (going outside the previous loop) as shown in (iii), inserts a new dot at E, and places a ring around both A and D, since both of these now have lines radiating from them in three directions.

The first player has now won because his opponent cannot join the two remaining dots (B and E) without crossing an existing line.

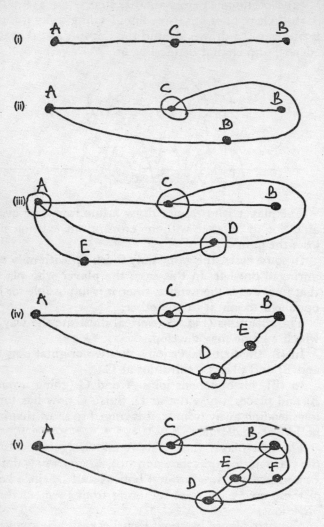

Fig. 5. Sprouts

Notice that if, instead of joining A and D, the first player had joined B and D, as shown in (iv), and had placed his new dot at E, the second player could have won by joining B and E after the manner shown in (v).

After having mastered the rudiments of the game, players can make it more involved by starting off with three dots in the form of a triangle, or four dots in the form of a square, instead of just the two dots described above.

Identikit

This pastime is based on the famous police method of piecing together faces, feature by feature, from descriptions given by a witness.

Fig. 6 shows a number of simple shapes for each of six different characteristics: shape of face, hair, eyes, nose, mouth, and accessories (such as spectacles or beard).

The idea is for one member of the party to act as 'witness'. His job is to think of some actual person (preferably one known to all members of the party) and to describe that person in words without actually revealing his or her identity. Each of the other members of the party selects from Fig. 6 the features he thinks most closely resemble the description given. Each then reproduces these features on a piece of paper as best he can – amending them slightly as he thinks necessary.

When all have finished, the witness reveals by name the identity of the 'wanted person', and the drawings are compared to see whose effort most closely resembles the person who was described.

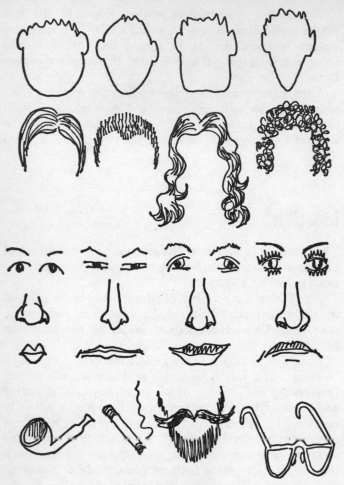

Fig. 6. Identikit

It is most unlikely that any of the efforts will very closely resemble the wanted person but a good deal of fun can result from examining a batch of what are probably very unflattering likenesses.

Wandering Minstrels

Some suggestions for musically-minded passengers.

Sing Song

Singing to the breeze is essentially a countryside diversion, and on the open road you can let yourselves go without disturbing anyone else.

Just in case you can't think of a song offhand, here are the titles of a few old favourites just to jog your

THREE BLIND MICE

memory (long before you have worked through them, someone will almost certainly be reminded of something else they want to sing): 'Little Bo-Peep', 'Three Blind Mice', 'Old Macdonald Had a Farm', 'John Brown's Body', 'It's a Long Way to Tipperary', 'One Man Went to Mow', 'Polly-Wolly Doodle', and 'Clementine'.

One at a Time Please

As a change from straight singing, try a musical competition, the object being to guess a well-known tune from the smallest number of notes.

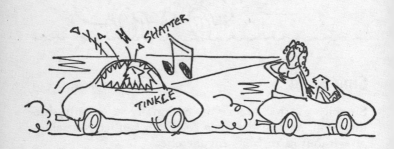

One of the party is appointed vocalist. He or she, as the case may be, then hums (or dah-de-dahs) the first two notes of some tune. If no one can guess correctly the tune the 'vocalist' has in mind, the first three notes are then hummed – then the first four notes, and so on until someone has identified the tune.

The player identifying the tune has the option of becoming vocalist for the next round or of naming someone else to do the humming.

I've Got Rhythm

This is another guessing competition based on the fact that most tunes have a distinctive rhythm which enables them to be identified by that alone.

One of the party privately decides upon some well-known tune, and then taps out the beat (by clapping the fingertips of one hand on the palm of the other) until someone identifies the tune correctly. The winner then becomes the 'musician' for the next round.

Can You Make It

Half a dozen easily constructed novelties that can be made either while travelling or during a roadside halt.

Fan

To make a *Fan*, you need a piece of paper which is roughly square (say about 12 inches each way). Newspaper or even a page torn from a magazine will serve admirably.

Crease the paper to and fro at regular intervals (with about half an inch between each fold) as shown in Fig. 7(i).

Halve the folded paper, making a sharp crease across the middle, and draw the two halves together as shown in (ii).

The two adjacent folds can be clipped together by making three short tears on the edges at the point A while holding the two halves together, and then folding back the two resulting tabs as shown in (iii).

The 'fan' may now be either opened out for use, or folded up for carrying in a breast pocket or handbag.

(i)

A

(ii)

(iii)

FAN
CLUB

Fig. 7. Fan

Admiral's Hat

A single page of newspaper is the ideal size and shape for the manufacture of an *Admiral's Hat*.

First halve the paper crosswise, by folding it forward along the dotted line AB in Fig. 8(i).

This will produce the shape shown in (ii).

Fold forward the two corners A and B to produce (iii), then fold up the shaded portion C to make (iv).

Turn the whole hat over, and fold up the dotted portion D to produce (v).

Insert the finger into the slot at the bottom edge and open up. The hat is now complete.

While he is about it, the hatter may as well make one hat for each member of the party. 'Admirals' hats' are useful holiday headgear, and make ideal face-covers to prevent sunburnt noses while snoozing on the beach.

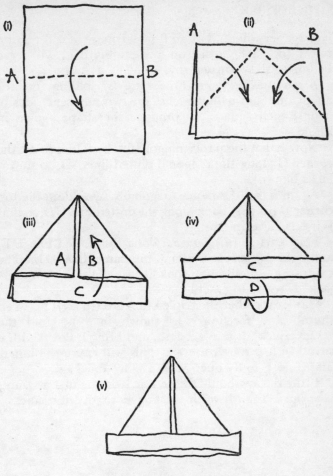

Fig. 8. Admiral's Hat

Crackerjack

Newspaper will do, but an 8-inch square of stiff writing paper (or paper torn from a shopping bag) will serve better for this amusing toy.

Begin making your *Crackerjack* by folding forward about one and a half inches on two adjacent sides of your 8-inch square, to produce the shape shown in Fig. 9.

Now halve the paper diagonally, by folding *back* the corner C along the diagonal dotted line AB, so that it looks like (ii).

Again halve the paper diagonally by folding the top corner B (in (ii)) back along the dotted line CD, so that B meets A, as in (iii).

Fold part A (iii) *forward* along the dotted line DE, and fold B *backward* along the same line DE. The contraption should now look like (iv), and the 'crackerjack' is ready to crack!

Gather together the triple tab ACB (in (iv)) between thumb and forefinger as shown in (v). Hold the 'crackerjack' at arm's length, and bring it down with a swift swish through the air. This will cause the innermost fold F to fly open with a sharp crack.

If the device should fail to crack on the first attempt, ease out F slightly with the fingers to give it a start.

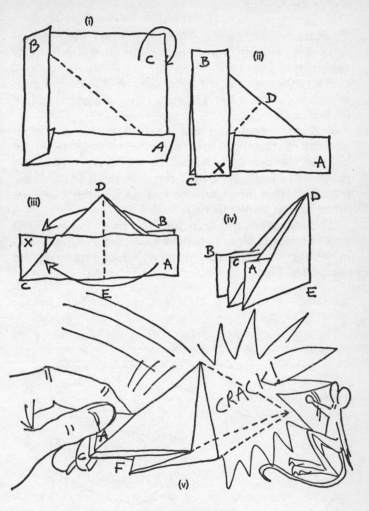

Fig. 9. Crackerjack

Frog-kerchief

To make a handkerchief 'frog', begin by rolling up two sides of a handkerchief to form a double-roll AB – CD as shown in Fig. 10(i).

Next fold over the left-hand third of the double roll, and then the right-hand third, so that the handkerchief looks like (ii).

Beginners may find the next operation easier to perform if they ask someone else to help them by holding the two ends A and C, while the frog-maker proceeds to push the end B through the middle of the frog from one side, and the end D through from the other side as shown in (iii).

The manufacturer then tugs the protruding ends B and D towards him, as his assistant tugs ends A and C in the opposite direction, as in (iv) which represents the completed frog.

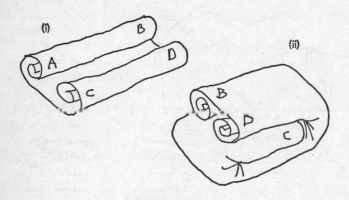

Fig. 10. Frog-kerchief

If tossed gently on to the lap, seat, or floor, the toy will land with a remarkably frog-like flop.

Helicopter

One of the simplest novelties that can be made from paper is the *Helicopter*. A piece of paper about 8 inches long by 2 inches wide is first halved down the middle, creasing it sharply.

It should then be neatly torn down the crease for a distance of about 2 inches and the two flaps thus formed should be opened out as in Fig. 11(i), again sharply creasing the line where the flaps open out.

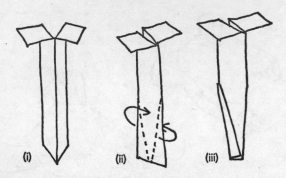

Fig. 11. Helicopter

The body should now be folded back and forth along the dotted lines shown in (ii), so that the completed 'helicopter' looks like (iii).

The helicopter is launched by throwing it upwards like a dart. At the top of its trajectory, it should turn over and descend with a spinning motion. A hair-clip slipped over the dart-end as additional weight can sometimes improve its flying abilities.

While adequate enough for the manufacture of *Helicopters*, the space available in the back seat of a car is too confined for test flights. You will therefore have to wait for a break in the journey before trying a launch.

Parachute

While on the subject of flight, you may also like to try your hand at constructing a *Parachute*, though again you will have to wait until the car stops before you have a chance to try it out.

You need a tissue (or a handkerchief) and four pieces of cotton, each about 16 inches long.

Tie one piece of cotton to each corner of the tissue, then knot together the four lengths of cotton about 4 inches from their ends as shown in Fig. 12.

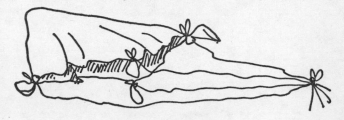

Fig. 12. Parachute

The bundle of loose ends is then used to tie on the 'parachutist', who is represented by a matchbox.

To launch the 'parachute', crumple the tissue gently together, and partly around the matchbox – then toss the whole bundle as high as it will go. If the matchbox should prove too light to drag the parachute open, load it with one or two pebbles.

Games after Dark

Sleep-inducing games for tired travellers.

MIDNIGHT GRAZING

Odd Tots

A mild degree of mental effort plus an element of monotony are the main ingredients of successful sleep-inducing pastimes.

In *Odd Tots* one person announces an *odd* number not greater than 5 (i.e. 1, 3, or 5). To this the next person adds another odd number not greater than 5, and this process continues, with the players claiming a win every time they can make the total ten or a multiple of ten.

For example, the game may proceed thus: '3 plus 1 makes 4, plus 5 makes 9, plus 1 makes 10 (that's a win), plus 3 makes 13, plus 5 makes 18, plus 3 makes 21, plus 1 makes 22, plus 5 makes 27, plus 3 makes 30 (that's another win) . . .' And so on.

After a while the game can become remarkably boring – but that is the whole point of the exercise!

Fuzz-Buzz

Another counting game which some people find interesting during the day, but sleep-inducing when played in the dark, is *Fuzz-Buzz*.

The players simply take it in turns to count up 'One . . . Two . . . Three . . . Four . . . Five . . .' etc., except that whenever one comes to a number which either ends in a three or is a multiple of three, he says 'Fuzz', and whenever he comes to a number which ends in a four or is a multiple of four, he says 'Buzz'.

Thus the count goes: 'One, Two, Fuzz, Buzz, Five, Fuzz, Seven, Buzz, Fuzz, Ten, Eleven, Fuzz-Buzz, Fuzz, Buzz, Fuzz, Buzz, Seventeen . . .' and so on. Thus twenty-four becomes 'Fuzz-Buzz-Buzz' because it is a multiple of both three and four, and also ends in a four.

After a few minutes of this sort of thing, the mind usually becomes quite fuzzy enough to welcome a little sleep.

Once Upon A Time

You don't really have to be very knowledgeable about fairy tales to entertain the children with this one. Indeed, the more often you go wrong the better, for the idea is to let the children spot mistakes, which should be as frequent as you can make them. For instance:

'Once upon a time, there was a little girl called Jack Horner.' Which should produce the response:

'Jack Horner wasn't a girl. He was a boy.'

'Well then, a little boy called Jack Horner, who had lost his sheep, and didn't know where to find them.'

'That was Little Bo-Peep.'

'Was it? Well, anyway, he had so many sheep he didn't know what to do.'

'You're getting it mixed up with the Old Woman who lived in a shoe.'

'Then I had better start again. Once upon a time there was a little boy called Bo-Peep.'

'Now you're wrong again.'

And so on.

Don't be alarmed if the first few responses are scathing. It usually doesn't take very long for the listener to give a drowsy sigh of exasperation, and seek refuge in sleep as the best way of escaping such a crazy world of unreality.

Proverbial Naps

Proverbs, which we have already met earlier in *Proverbial Fun*, can also be used as sleep-inducers. The technique is to repeat them with pauses (very long pauses) between each word. For instance: 'Don't ... cross ... your ... bridges ...'

By which time, if not before, someone should have guessed the remainder of the proverb (which is, of course, '... before you come to them').

Here are half a dozen to give you a start: 'He who laughs last laughs longest,' 'The longest way round is the surest way home,' 'Faint heart never won fair lady,' 'Spare the rod and spoil the child,' 'If wishes were horses, beggars would ride,' 'You cannot be in two places at the same time.'

LOOK BEFORE YOU SLEEP

The longer the pause between words, within reason, the better. It is sometimes an idea to pause so long that the listener thinks your mind has wandered off the subject, and that you need prompting – in which case, don't start the proverb again; just add the next word, in a tired, yawny sort of way.

Sheep on the Road

Counting sheep has been a traditional method of getting to sleep from time immemorial. At night, the approaching traffic may be used for the same purpose.

To give the game some point, suggest seeing how long it will take to count up to, say, 200 cars while watching the headlights of the approaching traffic. A steadily approaching stream of lights has a mildly mesmeric effect, and if the eyes get tired, the counter

may as well shut them while trying to keep count by
listening for the swish of the passing vehicles.

If you have a radio or cassette-recorder in the car, a
little soft background music can also add to the drowsy
effect.

Humpty-Dumpty

When it comes to sleep-inducing games, there are some
who swear that this is the most effective of them all. It
consists simply of repeating a nursery rhyme by saying
the first word, then the first and second words, then
the first second and third words, and so on. For
example, 'Humpty-Dumpty' comes out like this:
'Humpty – Humpty-Dumpty – Humpty-Dumpty sat –
Humpty-Dumpty sat on – Humpty-Dumpty sat on a –
Humpty-Dumpty sat on a wall – Humpty-Dumpty sat
on a wall Humpty – Humpty-Dumpty . . .'

And so on.

If you make a mistake, you have to go right back to

137

the beginning and start all over again – which is really a frightful bore.

The monotonous repetition has a distinctly soporific effect.

The winner is the first person to drop off to sleep!

PART THREE:
WHEN YOU GET THERE

*Games and pastimes suitable either for
holidays, or prolonged breaks in a journey
or an afternoon spent on the beach*

Shells and Pebbles

Games of mental skill in which shells or pebbles are used as counters.

Pebble-kayles

This is probably the simplest of the games that can be played with shells and pebbles. Even so, if you are intent on winning it calls for considerable foresight.

Twelve pebbles of roughly equal size (say about one inch in diameter) are arranged in the form of a ring. They should be closely placed so that each one is actually touching its neighbours.

The two players now take it in turns to claim either:

(a) One pebble from the ring

or

(b) Two *touching* pebbles

The game continues until all the pebbles have been claimed.

The winner is not the person who collects most pebbles, but the one who legitimately claims the *last* pebble (or pair of touching pebbles) from the ring.

Either or Both

This is another game in which the winner is the one who manages to claim the last pebble (or legitimate group of pebbles) from the ground, but the strategy called for is quite different from that needed in the game of *Pebble-kayles*.

A handful of pebbles (say about ten or fifteen) are arbitrarily divided into two *unequal* piles by one of the players. The two opponents then take it in turns to draw pebbles from the two piles – the player who did not distribute them having first draw.

At each draw a player may take either:

(a) *Any number* of pebbles from *one* of the two piles

or

(b) *An equal number* of pebbles from *both* the two piles.

Notice that the first player to draw could, if he wished, claim *all* the pebbles from one pile, but he would be ill-advised to do so, for his opponent could then win by claiming *all* the pebbles from the other pile.

As with all pebble-claiming games, though easy enough to play, the contest calls for real skill when one is matched against a wily opponent.

Shelection

This is the most subtle of all the games in which two players have to claim objects from the ground.

Although pebbles may be used (provided you can find three different types of pebble, each easily distinguishable by size, shape or colour) shells are preferable since different kinds of shell are more easily distinguishable than different kinds of pebble.

To begin with you need about fifteen or twenty shells, and this collection must include three different varieties. For instance, six winkles, eight mussels, and five scallops would do.

All the shells are then placed together in a single pile on the ground, and the two players take it in turns to claim as many shells as they like, provided that on each turn the shells claimed are *all of one variety*. A player is not permitted to claim two or more shells of a different variety on the same turn.

Each player *must* claim at least one shell on each turn, and the person who picks up the last remaining shell is *the loser*. The strategy is therefore to claim shells in such a way that your opponent is left with the task of claiming the last shell.

Three Men's Morris

This must surely be one of the oldest games in the world, for it was played in ancient Egypt, Greece, and Rome, as well as in China and amongst the Red Indians of North America.

One player has three shells, and his opponent three pebbles (though two different types of shell or two types of pebble could be used to distinguish the players' pieces from one another).

Nine small holes are scooped out in the ground or sand, in the form of a square, as shown in Fig. 13.

Fig. 13. Three Men's Morris

The players now take it in turns to place their pieces one at a time into any of the nine holes. The object is (as in *Noughts and Crosses*) to get three of one's pieces in a line (either horizontally, vertically, or diagonally) but since the two opponents each have only three pieces, a player is careless indeed if he allows his opponent to get three in a line at this early stage of the game. If the opponent does get three in a line, he wins without more ado, but if neither player gets three in a line, the opponents continue to take it in turns, each moving one piece to a new hole at each turn.

The pieces may move only to an adjacent hole (either horizontally, vertically, or diagonally) at each turn. A piece cannot leap over an unoccupied hole or over another piece. Neither can it move into a hole already occupied by another piece.

As already said, the player who first succeeds in manoeuvring all his three pieces into a line is the winner.

Sheep and Goats

This is a *Patience* game, for it is played by one player. If one wants to introduce a competitive element, then the various members of a party can each try it out with a view to seeing who can complete the game in the fewest number of moves.

Three light-coloured pebbles (or shells) and three dark-coloured pebbles are placed in seven holes scooped out in a line in the ground as shown in Fig. 14.

Fig. 14. Sheep and Goats

The light pebbles on the left are intended to represent a flock of sheep and the dark pebbles on the right a flock of goats. The two flocks wish to pass, but the lane is so narrow that no animal can squeeze past another.

An animal can, however, move forward one hole at a time, or it can leap over *one* other animal, provided there is a vacant hole beyond for it to land in. It cannot leap over more than one other animal in a single move.

The object of the player is to move the animals according to these rules so that the three goats finish up in the left-hand holes formerly occupied by the sheep, and vice versa.

Beach Solitaire

As its name suggests, this is another game for a solitary player. It poses quite a tricky problem.

Two shells and two pebbles are placed at the corners of a square formed by scooping out nine holes in the ground. The shells are placed in the two corners furthest from the player, and the pebbles in the two corners nearest to him, as shown in Fig. 15.

The object is for the two shells and the two pebbles to exchange places, so that the shells are now in the two near corners, and the pebbles in the two far corners.

On every turn a piece must move exactly one hole

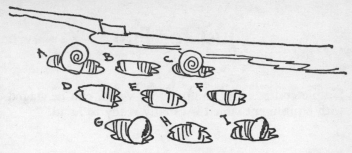

Fig. 15. Beach Solitaire

'on the square' (i.e. horizontally or vertically) *and* one hole diagonally. Thus the shell in hole C (in Fig. 15) could move either to hole D or H, while the pebble in hole G could move to either F or B. (Chess players will recognize this sort of move as the leap which the knight executes every time he moves.)

Once again, the aim of the player should be to accomplish the change-over of shells for pebbles in the least possible number of moves.

Just for Fun

Simple contests and competitions which can be staged with equipment which is usually ready to hand.

Sandstorm

While a beach is obviously the ideal place for staging this amusing contest, any level, open space without obstructions will do. The contest is intended to illustrate the plight of a traveller who has been caught in a desert sandstorm which reduces visibility to zero.

A circle about 6 feet in diameter is marked out on the ground to represent 'Home Sweet Home'. The 'traveller' stands in the centre of this circle, and is blind-folded.

He is now given a series of instructions which he must follow. For instance, he may be told to walk ten paces north, then eight paces east, then three paces south. Each of these paces must be full-length strides. From the point where he finishes up, he must then (still blindfolded) find his way back 'Home' – either by retracing the steps he made, or by heading directly for where he thinks Home is.

When he thinks that he is once more back in the circle he halts, and the blindfold is removed so that he can see how well or badly he has fared. Each member of the party takes it in turn to play the role of traveller.

A variation of this game is for two circles to be drawn – the Home circle (about six feet in diameter as before) and a larger circle (about fifteen feet or so in diameter) near by. This larger circle represents an alligator-infested swamp. The traveller is then allowed to stand on the far side of the swamp and view the terrain before being blindfolded and required to find his way back Home. He 'dies' if any part of his foot touches the swamp, or if, when he halts, he is not within the Home circle.

Uh-huh

For this contest, the players are divided into teams consisting of two players each. One of the two players in each team is then blindfolded, and is required to negotiate an obstacle course consisting of camp-stools, hampers, coats laid on the ground (or whatever other suitable objects are to hand).

The role of the un-blindfolded player is to guide his 'blind' partner through this maze of obstacles, using only the phrase 'Uh-huh', spoken in whatever tone of voice seems appropriate. For instance, the 'blind man' may be warned that he is in danger of colliding with an obstacle by a short, incisive 'Uh-huh!', or encouraged, when he is on the right track, by a reassuring and leisurely 'Uh – huh', spoken with a lilt in the voice.

On completing the course, the pair swap roles, the guide becoming the blind man and vice versa. The new

blind man must then complete the return trip through the obstacles back to the original starting point. Every time a competitor bumps into or brushes against one of the obstacles, that counts as a 'fault' against the team.

If a watch with a second hand is available, then time can be introduced into the game to decide which team is the winner, in the event of two or more teams finishing with the same number of faults.

An amusing variation is for all the 'blind men' to walk the course simultaneously while their partners stand at the end of the course 'Uh-huh-hing'. Each blind man then has to distinguish by the sound of the voice whether an 'Uh-huh' is intended for him or for some other person.

Spectators should not be forbidden from saying 'Uh-ha-ha-ha-ha'. Very often they can't help it!

Fly Casting

A key (or any other small metal object which can be *securely* tied) is attached to a piece of string about 10–12 feet long. The other end of the string should then be tied to a stick (which itself should be about 4–5 feet long).

An empty beer can or similar target is placed roughly as far from the 'angler' as the string is long, and competitors take it in turns to try to lob the key on the target – using the sort of action normally employed by an angler. The first to strike the target with the key is the winner of the round.

Spectators should keep well away from the angler when he is casting, and should stand to the side of him rather than behind him!

Twiddle-twigs

This contest imitates a horse-race, the horses being empty milk bottles, matchboxes, or whatever other suitable items are to hand. A piece of string, cotton, or wool about 6 feet long is attached to each 'horse', and the other end of the string is tied tightly around a twig which should be about the thickness of a pencil. To be fair, all contestants' twigs should be of about the same diameter.

The contestants (or 'jockeys') then stand in a row,

their horses being lined up some distance away as far as the string will allow.

At the starting signal, the jockeys commence winding their horses in towards them by twiddling the twigs round and round between their fingers, thus winding up the string.

The winner is, of course, the person who first manages to wind his horse right in until it is touching his twig. The secret of success is to keep the coil of string building up on itself, thus increasing the effective diameter of the twig. In this way, later turns of the twig will draw in more string than the early ones.

Egg Flip

This simple game of skill can be played either in the open or inside, for it requires very little space.

To play it one needs five bottle-tops, and the bottom half of a paper-pulp egg-box of the kind in which eggs are commonly sold by the half-dozen.

The box should be placed about 5 feet away from the players, with its end (not its side) towards them, as shown in Fig. 16.

The first player now tosses the five bottle-tops, one at a time, in an attempt to lob them into the egg-box. The bottle-top should be launched by balancing it on the back of one's outstretched fingers which should be held together to form a launching platform.

Fig. 16. Egg-Flip

A bottle-top landing in one of the two nearest holes scores one point, in one of the two middle holes two points, and in one of the two furthest holes three points, as shown in the diagram.

After a player's score has been totalled for his five tosses, the bottle-tops are retrieved, and passed on to the other players to compete in turn.

Naturally, the winner scoring the greatest number of points wins the game.

Ducks and Drakes

This most venerable of country pastimes can be played wherever there is a river, lake, or other stretch of smooth water. It can also be played at the edge of the sea provided the water is not too choppy.

The contestants take turns to see who can skip a stone across the water the greatest number of times. Success depends not only on the throw (which should be low and with a backward spinning motion) but also on the careful selection of one's missiles. Very flat stones usually

skip well, but it is surprising how well a plump, egg-shaped stone will skip when expertly thrown.

Since distances are difficult to compare, the winner is usually regarded as the one who can achieve the most skips with a single throw. Individual skips can usually be counted fairly easily.

Beach Games

Games which can add fun to a stroll along the beach, or to an afternoon spent on the sands.

Father's Footsteps

This is a very simple way to derive a little added amusement from a family walk along the sands.

One of the party acts as 'father', and he leads the way along the beach, varying his stride by occasionally leaping forwards, sideways, or even backwards. The other members of the party, following in line, are expected to follow directly in father's footsteps.

There are no scores, winners, or losers. The whole thing is just for fun, but if you want a criterion of success, a footstep may be reckoned as well founded, so long as any part of an imprint impinges on any part of the imprint left by someone in front.

Every hundred yards or so father should retire to the back of the queue, and let the next in line succeed.

Drake's Bowls

If Sir Francis Drake's bowl had rolled into the sea, would England have suffered defeat at the hands of the Armada? We shall never know, but if your bowl rolls into the sea while you are playing *Drake's Bowls*, it will count as a defeat.

To play *Drake's Bowls* you need a beach which slopes just enough for a ball (once it is moving) to roll towards the sea of its own accord.

The 'bowler' stands about 20 feet from the water's edge, and facing along the beach. Ten or twelve feet ahead of him (and also about 20 feet from the water's edge) stands a second player called the 'boundaryman'.

The bowler bowls his ball (any sort of ball from a golf ball to a beach ball will do) along the beach more or less parallel to the sea, *but between the boundaryman and the water*. The bowler then sets off to chase the ball, allowing it to run as far as he dares before it reaches the water. If the ball reaches the water before he has picked it up, that bowl is disqualified, and the turn passes to the next player.

The object is to see how far one can bowl the ball subject to the rules described above. The faster the ball is bowled, the farther it will go, but the harder the bowler must run if he is to prevent its reaching the water's edge.

The game can be played progressively during a family walk along the beach. In this case, each bowl is made from a point opposite the place where the previous bowl was stopped, and again about 20 feet from the water's edge. When playing 'progressive' bowls, individual efforts can be compared by someone pacing out each bowling attempt.

Cherry Toppler

Build a sandcastle about 8 or 10 inches high, and place on top of it a round pebble which should be about an inch in diameter.

The players now take it in turns to scoop away sand from the castle, using a spoon or an empty seashell. The idea is to avoid dislodging the stone, but to leave the structure in such a condition that your opponent's next scoop will send the stone 'cherry' toppling.

If the contestants are overcautious and inclined to take such small 'bites' that the game could go on for hours, a rule may be introduced that, on each bite a player must take sufficient sand to fill some small container such as a plastic mug or empty ice-cream tub.

Buried Treasure

A never-failing way to amuse children on the beach is to draw a circle about 8 feet in diameter on the sand, and (while no one is looking) to bury half a dozen wrapped toffees or chocolates at different places within the circle.

The sweets should be buried about 2 or 3 inches below the surface, and when burying is complete, the sand all over the circle should be smoothed by hand to remove all traces of the burying.

The family is then told how many sweets have been buried, and invited to excavate for the 'buried treasure'.

Pin-weed

There are few beaches on which one cannot find a few sticks and a few strands of seaweed with which to play *Pin-weed*.

Plant three twigs in the sand in a straight line, and about 3 feet apart from one another. The first stick should have about 18 inches of it exposed, while the middle stick and last stick should be exposed to heights of about 12 inches and 6 inches respectively.

The 'pitcher', equipped with three strands of seaweed, now stands about 12 feet away from the first stick, and in line with all three of them as shown in Fig. 17.

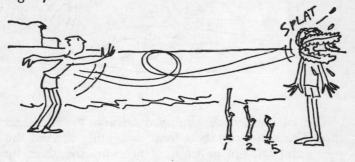

Fig. 17. Pin-Weed

His object is to lob the strands of seaweed, one at a time, so that they wrap themselves around the sticks. If the seaweed comes to rest against the closest stick it counts as one point – if it clears the first stick and comes to rest against the middle stick it scores two points, and if it lands against the furthest stick five points are scored.

Each player has three lobs at each turn, and the winner is the one who first achieves a total score of, say, twenty points.

Sand Fishing

A rough circle about 8–10 feet in diameter is scratched in the sand to represent the fish-pond. In the centre of the circle are placed half a dozen or so assorted objects such as plastic mugs, empty cans, or empty ice-cream tubs to represent the fish.

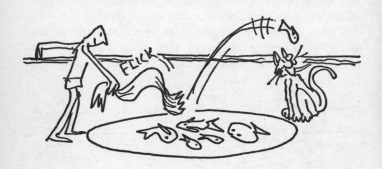

The players, each equipped with a towel, stand spaced at equal distances from each other around the pond, and attempt to fish the objects towards them by flicking with their towels. A player may lean over to secure his catch when it has been whipped close enough to be within reach, but is not permitted to set either foot or hand on the surface of the pond. There is no reason why a player should not try to land a 'fish' already whipped close to him by a fellow-angler, but players are not permitted to move around the pond once the fishing has started. Each must stick to his original position at the pond's edge until the fishing has been completed.

The winner is, of course, the contestant who manages to land most fish.

Beach Golf

A beach, with its acres of sand for the making of bunkers and other hazards, is the ideal spot to lay out a miniature golf course.

There is no need to go in for a full eighteen-hole course – half a dozen holes should be enough for a bit of fun. The holes (each of which should be about 4 inches in diameter) should be spaced roughly 10–20 feet apart. The holes may be simply scooped out in the sand, or, if you want a more elegant course, empty ice-cream buckets can be sunk into the sand up to their rims. Bunkers, ridges, and gullies can be formed by digging out or piling up sand at various spots along the course.

Any sort of ball which is small enough to fit into the holes will do instead of a golf-ball. As for clubs, a walking stick, the handle of a sandcastle spade, or any suitably sized piece of driftwood should do.

In the Groove

Using either one's hands, a sandcastle bucket, or the edge of a plastic picnic plate, gouge out in the sand a groove some 20 feet or so long, about 6 inches wide and 2 or 3 inches deep. The groove should not be straight, but should wander about serpentine fashion with at

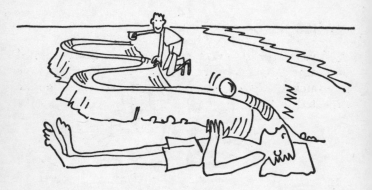

least half a dozen bends in it. The surface of the groove should be as smooth as you can reasonably make it; that is why the edge of a plastic plate is probably the best tool to work with when constructing it.

A tennis ball (or any ball of a similar size) is now placed at one end of the groove, and contestants take it in turns to see who can negotiate the course in the fewest number of strokes. The ball has to be propelled along the groove by striking it with one's clenched knuckles.

If at any time the ball should be struck out of the groove that counts as a stroke against the player, and the ball has to be returned to the place from which it was struck.

The course can be made more complicated by making short blind alleys (especially at corners) into which the ball may run, thus causing the player to lose a stroke by having to play out of the blind alley back on to the main course. Again, bypasses may be provided at one or two spots along the route, so that when a player comes to a junction he must use his judgement in deciding which of the alternative routes is likely to prove most easily negotiable.

Bucket Race

For this competition each competitor must be equipped with an empty ice-cream tub (or plastic mug) to serve as a bucket, and with an empty bottle which he will be expected to fill.

The players line up about 20 yards from the water's edge, with buckets in hand and bottles set firmly in the sand beside them.

At the word 'Go' they run for the sea, fill their buckets, and return to empty the water they have fetched into the bottle. Several journeys to and fro will be necessary before the bottle is filled, and the first runner to get his bottle brim-full is the winner.

If there should happen to be a large party (say eight or more people) the players can be divided into two teams. In this case only one bucket and one bottle is needed for each team. Each team then forms a 'fireman's chain' between the water's edge and its bottle, passing bucketfuls of water along the chain until its bottle is full.

Ball Games

A ball is an essential item of equipment on any holiday outing, but there is no real need to carry around an assortment of balls for different games. Playing a game with a ball which is the wrong size and weight can sometimes add to the fun. A beach ball or tennis ball will serve for most games, and even if you haven't got that you can improvise: a tightly wound ball of string or wool is ideal for many games. Failing that, an empty plastic 'lemon' or an inflated balloon with a little water inside it for added weight can add novelty to a game simply by the way they wobble. As a last resort, wrap a light pebble in a ball of tightly crumpled paper, and bind it together with a few strips of adhesive tape, or simply stuff a brown-paper bag tight with crumpled paper.

Penalty Ball

Throwing a ball to one another while standing in a ring is probably the simplest sort of ball game one can think of, but a touch of novelty can be added to it by awarding penalties for each dropped catch.

Each time a player drops a ball he is penalized as follows:

First Miss: He must play (i.e. both catch and throw) with one hand only, though it does not matter which hand (left or right) he uses.

Second Miss: He may use both hands, but must play kneeling.

Third Miss: He must play with only one hand while kneeling.

Fourth Miss: He may use both hands, but play while sitting.

Fifth Miss: He must play with only one hand from a sitting position.

Sixth Miss: He is out.

If, while in one of the penalty positions, a player does manage to catch a ball in the prescribed manner, he regains one step on the penalty ladder. Thus if he manages to catch the ball while playing in the '*Third Miss*' position, he goes back to the '*Second Miss*' position.

The game can be staged as a competition, the winner being the last person remaining after all the others have gone out as the result of a '*Sixth Miss*'.

Skittle-cans

Empty drink-cans make ideal pins for a game of skittles.

Six or ten cans should be arranged in a triangular formation, with each can about 3 or 4 inches from its immediate neighbours. The apex of the triangle should point towards the bowler, who should take up his position on a line drawn about 20 feet away.

The 'bowler' is now given three balls. There is no need for the balls to be all of the same size; an odd assortment of balls (such as a tennis ball, a cricket ball, and a beach ball) can add to the fun.

The bowler then tries to knock over the cans by throwing, tossing, or bowling his balls one at a time. He scores one point for every can that finishes up on its side.

The cans are then rearranged, and the three balls passed to the next contestant for him to try his luck at bowling.

Knock-out

Any fairly hard, smooth patch of ground will do for this ball game. A ring about 3 feet in diameter is drawn on the ground. The two contestants position themselves on opposite sides of the ring, and about 5 or 6 yards away from it. In the centre of the ring is placed a target which may be an empty drink-can, plastic mug, or similar object.

One of the players now takes a tennis ball (or any sort of ball with a reasonable amount of bounce) and throws it with the object of knocking the target outside the ring.

If the ball is cleanly fielded by his opponent, it is now the second player's turn to aim for the target if it is still anywhere in the ring. If the non-thrower fails to field the ball cleanly (i.e. if it runs past him and he has to chase it) he must return the ball to the thrower who is entitled to another shot.

The player whose shot finally knocks the target clear of the ring is the winner.

Bing-bong

Bing-bong is played with tennis rackets and tennis balls, but with no net.

Two circles, each about 12 feet in diameter, and about 10 feet apart are scratched out in the ground to represent the courts.

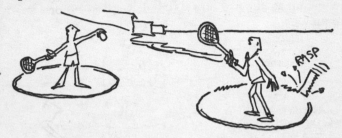

Underhand strokes only arc allowed, and a player gains one point if his opponent fails to return correctly a ball which has landed in his court. If a return (or service) lands outside a court, that is a point to the receiver provided his racket has not touched the ball.

Change of service and scoring is as in *Ping-pong*. The service changes whenever the two opposing scores together total a multiple of five, and the winner is the first player to achieve a total of twenty-one points.

French Cricket

This venerable game is played with a cricket bat (or similar piece of wood) and a tennis ball (or any ball which bounces well, and is not so hard that it will hurt your shins).

The batsman stands with his legs together, protecting his legs by placing his bat in front of them. The fieldsmen (any in number) surround him, and attempt to hit

the batsman's legs with a ball. The batsman is not
allowed to move his legs during his innings, and must
therefore ward off shots from behind him by twisting
his body in that direction.

The fieldsman who fields the ball becomes the bowler
for the next throw, and must throw the ball from the
spot at which he fielded it. However, no fieldsman may
come up to closer than three bat-lengths from the batsman.

The batsman is out, either if his legs are struck by the
ball, or if a fieldsman catches on the full any stroke from
the bat.

The bowler who bowls the batsman out, or the
fieldsman who catches him out, becomes the next batsman irrespective of how many innings he has already
had.

'Runs' may be scored by the batsman passing the
bat around his body, each time the bat is passed around
counting as one run.

Anglecourt

The courts for this 'singles' game are marked out on the
ground as shown in Fig. 18. The forecourts should be

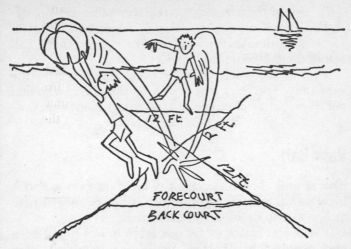

Fig. 18. Anglecourt

about 12 feet long on each side, and the backcourts are presumed to extend indefinitely.

Each of the two players stands in his own backcourt, and is not permitted to enter the forecourt while the ball is in play.

The server (standing in his backcourt) throws the ball (which should preferably be a largish one like a beach ball) in such a way that it should land in his opponent's forecourt. The receiver must try to catch it and return it by throwing it into the server's forecourt. The rally continues until the ball either:

(a) Fails to land in the forecourt to which it is thrown,
    or

(b) lands in the forecourt, but bounces twice in that forecourt,
    or

(c) lands in the forecourt, but bounces outside the backcourt.

In any of these cases, the receiver gains one point.

The thrower gains a point if the receiver fails to catch a legitimate throw on the first bounce as the ball leaves the forecourt.

The loser of each point becomes the server for the next rally, and the game is won by the player who first achieves a clear three-point lead over his opponent.

Pass Ball

This is probably the simplest of all team games, and is ideal as a family recreation since it can be played with as few as two members to each team.

The object is simply for one team to toss a ball from one member to another, while the opposing team attempts to intercept it in flight. No tackling is allowed,

and a player must throw the ball from the position in which he was standing when he caught it.

There is usually no scoring in the game, but the team which manages to achieve the greatest number of consecutive passes without interception during the course of the game can consider itself as having proved its superiority.

Handball

Two goals (each about 8 feet wide) are marked out on the ground, using sticks, buckets, camp-stools, or whatever else is to hand for goal-posts.

The object of the two opponents (or two opposing teams) is now to strike a soft ball (such as a tennis ball or beach ball) so that it rolls between the goal-posts of the opposing side.

Players are allowed to use only their clenched fists for striking the ball. If at any time a player should grasp the ball, that counts as a 'foul', and a free strike is awarded to the other team. This means that one of its members is allowed to strike the ball from wherever the foul occurred, while all the players of the offending team have to stand back and not interfere with the attempt to score a goal.

After a goal has been scored the ball is returned to the centre of the field where it is bounced or thrown up to restart the game.

If the ball goes behind a goal line without passing between the posts, it is thrown back into play by a member of the team defending that goal – and for this throw he is permitted to grasp the ball in his hand, but must throw from a kneeling position.

After ten minutes' play, the teams change ends for a second half, also of ten minutes. The winning team is the one which scores most goals during the two halves added together.

Foot Rounders

An equilateral triangle (with each side about 10 yards long) is marked out on the ground, and a circle (about 6 feet in diameter) is drawn around each corner. These circles are called 'bases', and from one of them (which is designated 'home base') a baseline is extended indefinitely on each side as shown in Fig. 19.

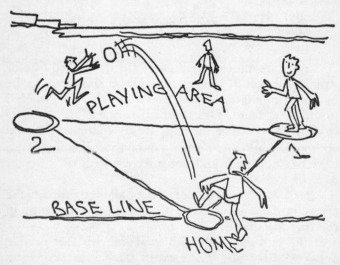

Fig. 19. Foot Rounders

The players are divided into two teams, and the toss of a coin decides which shall have first innings.

The fielding team spreads itself out around the playing area, but outside the triangle. (In practice, one fieldsman is usually placed somewhere near each base.)

The 'first man in' of the kicking team places the ball on the ground inside the home base, and kicks it as far as he can into the playing area. If his kick goes astray and finishes up behind the base line he is out straight away. If the ball goes anywhere in the triangle or the playing area, the kicksman must immediately run for 'first base', and if he thinks there is time, he may continue on to 'second base', and thence back to home base. Whenever the kicksman runs, any of his team who happen to be standing on first or second base must also run, since two kicksmen are not permitted to occupy the same base at the same time.

Meanwhile, when a fieldsman retrieves the ball (for which purpose he is permitted to enter or cross the triangle) he must either run towards any base for which one of the opposing team is heading, or throw the ball to a fieldsman standing near or on that base. If the ball is grounded in the base before the runner has reached it, that runner is out.

On reaching the home base without having been run out, a kicksman scores one run for his side – unless he has managed to complete the whole circuit off a single kick, in which case this counts as a 'homer' and scores three runs.

When each member of the kicking team has had one kick, that team's innings is complete, and it is the fielding team's turn to kick.

A match consists of two innings for each side – the aggregate runs scored by a team for the whole match deciding the winners.

Chunnel Ball

This game is a variation of *Tunnel Ball*, but it is called
'*Chunnel Ball*' because the tunnel formed by the
players' legs is, like the Channel Tunnel, a long-distance
one. The game is suitable only for larger parties
numbering six or more, since it does need at least three
players to each competing team. On the other hand,
six is about as many as can be comfortably accom-
modated in a team under ordinary playing conditions –
for a fair amount of space is another prerequisite for the
contest.

The contest begins like ordinary *Tunnel Ball*, the
players in each team lining up one behind another, and
with their legs astride.

At the word 'Go!' the front member of each team
bowls the ball between his legs, the players behind him
passing it in turn between their legs until it reaches the
person at the back who picks it up. And now comes the
difference from ordinary *Tunnel Ball*. Instead of running
just to the head of his team, the man who picks up the

ball runs as far ahead of the team as he thinks is safe. There he bowls the ball between his legs, and again his team-mates behind guide and speed the ball on its way between their legs, to be picked up once again by the rear member of the team. But in doing this they must not stir from their positions.

If at any time the ball should fail to reach a member of the team, or if it should go wide, the *front* man must chase back, pick it up, and run ahead again for another attempt. Success therefore depends on judging how far ahead of your team you dare to run. Too short a distance, and you may lose ground to your opponents; too great a distance and you risk the ball going wide, which results in a delay.

The chunnelling continues until after, say, one minute, the time-keeper calls 'Halt!' The winning team is then the one whose *rearmost* man is farthest advanced from the starting-line.

Races

Suggestions for novel and entertaining races which can be staged with only a small number of competitors.

Open and Handicap

The chief difficulty with family races is the wide disparity of performance between the contestants. Neither six-year-old Julie nor sixty-year-old grandpa stands much chance against sixteen-year-old John. One can give Julie and grandpa a start on John, but how much of a start?

One way of settling this question is to stage a race in two parts – first an 'Open' championship, and then a 'Handicap' race. The two-in-one race is staged this way.

For the Open event all the sprinters line up at the starting post, with the starter-cum-judge (if there is one) taking his hand at the finishing line (which can be anything from fifty to a hundred yards away).

On the word 'Go!' they all run for the finishing line, but the moment the winner reaches it, the judge (or the winner himself if there is no judge) cries 'Stop!' All competitors must then halt instantly at the spots which they have reached.

Having thus settled who is the winner of the Open championship, the whole field then about-turns, each remaining at the place he or she has reached during the Open event. Now for the Handicap: on the word 'Go!' they all sprint back to the original starting post which now becomes the finishing line for the Handicap, and the first to cross the line this time is declared winner of the Handicap. With a bit of luck it should prove to be a very close and exciting finish. Provided everyone has played fair, and has run as fast as he can in an attempt to win the Open championship, the subsequent Handicap race should result in the whole field crossing the finishing line almost at the same time, with Julie and grandpa having virtually the same chance of winning as John.

Here and There

This is a race in which, if the fast ones are going to win they may have to overtake the slow ones quite a few times.

Two finishing lines should be drawn about 50 or 60 yards apart. The runners then line up half-way between these two lines, while the starter stands at one or other of the lines. The finishing line at which the starter stands is called 'Here', and the other finishing line is called 'There'.

The starter then calls out 'Here!' and the runners must then sprint towards the line named. However, before they reach it, the starter cries 'There!', whereupon the entire field must turn and start sprinting for that line. They must again reverse the direction in which they are running whenever the starter changes his call. It is no good for runners to dawdle in expectation of a call, for until the race is finished no one knows which of the two lines will ultimately prove to be the finishing line.

The first person to cross the line towards which the field happens to be running at the moment is the winner, and he should announce that the race is over by crying 'Here!' or 'There!' (as the case may be) the moment he crosses the line.

The starter's calls should be randomly spaced. The fairest way to achieve this is for him to adopt some procedure such as flipping a coin and changing his call whenever the spin changes from heads to tails or vice versa. Another way to achieve random spacing of calls is for the starter to read to himself an item from a newspaper, magazine, or book, and change the call whenever he comes to the end of a sentence.

My Son John

> *Diddle diddle dumpling, my son John,*
> *He went to bed with his trousers on,*
> *One shoe off and one shoe on,*
> *Diddle diddle dumpling, my son John.*

So goes the nursery rhyme which describes this race. The race begins with all the competitors seated on the ground behind the starting line, wearing their shoes. On the word 'Go', each must take off his left shoe (and sock, if any) then, carrying the shoe with him, race with one shoe off and one shoe on for another line which should be about 25 yards away. On reaching this line the runner must *lie* down and, while in the prone

position, replace his left shoe and remove his right one. As soon as he has done this he must (without further orders) regain his feet and race back to the starting point, carrying his shoe with him, sit down, and replace his shoe.

The first person to stand up wearing both shoes is the winner.

As You Like It

Twenty or thirty metres is probably a long enough course for this race (or perhaps, one should say, series of races) because contestants are expected to shuttle back and forth several times before finally regaining the starting line, which serves also as a finishing post.

The idea is that each length of the course should be completed in some unusual, stipulated manner, for

instance: *hopping on one foot, running backwards, running on all fours*, or *running on all fours, but with the body facing upwards*.

The winner of each length is usually entitled to name the method of running to be adopted for the next length. Alternatively, each member of the party has one turn at prescribing the way in which the lengths should be run, in which case there will be as many lengths to the race as there are contestants.

Silly Sprints

Novelty may be added to a race by imposing on the runners practically any rule which will handicap their speed. Here are a few suggestions:

Egg and Spoon This is so well known that it scarcely needs description, but you should remember that it is

not necessary to have eggs (either real or china) in order to stage the race. Any roundish object such as a ball or an orange will do as a substitute for the egg. And if spoons are not available, the object to be carried may be balanced on the back of outstretched fingers.

Persian Market Another 'balancing' race inspired by eastern women who are so adept at carrying jars on their heads. In a family contest the 'jar' may be represented by a book, a matchbox, an empty drink can, or whatever else is to hand. The course should be fairly short – about twenty-five yards.

Legging It The runners have to complete the course while gripping an empty can, bottle, or similar object, between their legs. The can must be supported between the legs not higher than the knee. If it slips lower the runner must continue with the can in its new position. If the can should fall to the ground, the runner must return to the starting point and set off again. A course of 12 or 15 yards is long enough for an entertaining race.

Hobbledehoy In this race, the runner must hobble from start to finish while grasping each ankle firmly with one hand.

A Clean Pair of Heels

A clean and moderately dry beach is the ideal setting for this race.

Two parallel lines about 20 yards apart are scratched in the sand to represent the starting and finishing lines.

Each competitor is provided with a towel which he must place with its *rear edge* on the starting line.

At the word 'Go!' the runners step on to their towels and race for the finishing line, but at no time must their bare feet come into contact with the sand. Having stepped on to the towel, the runner must then skew the back half of the towel forward to provide a footing for the next step.

The winner is the first person to get any part of his towel over the finishing line, and is able to display a clean pair of heels as evidence that he did not step off his towel.

Entering Two by Two

There are several amusing races in which the competitors enter as pairs instead of as individual contestants.

Three-legged Race The left ankle of one runner is tied (by rope, belt, towel, or what-have-you) to the right ankle of his partner, so that they must race with their feet moving in unison.

Back-to-Back Race The two runners forming a team stand back to back, linking themselves together by passing their arms backwards around each other's waist – and must complete the course without breaking this grip.

Wheelbarrow Race One of each team acts as navvy by grasping the ankles of his partner who supports himself on his hands, face downwards, imitating a barrow. The navvy runs while the 'barrow' walks on his hands. On completing the course it is usual for the partners to swap roles for a return journey.

Leapfrog Each team proceeds by vaulting over one another's backs alternately. On landing, the player who

THUMP

has just vaulted must remain in the position where he landed, from where he must in turn be vaulted by his partner. So the race proceeds until one of the partners has reached the finishing line.

Stepping Stones A double sheet of newspaper is halved, halved again, then folded in three so that it forms a wad of twelve thicknesses measuring about 12 inches by 6 inches. Two such 'stepping stones' are provided for each team. One of the team runs while his partner positions the two stepping stones in front of him, picking up the rearmost stone after each pace and carrying it ahead for the runner to step (or leap) on to. Every pace the runner takes must be on to a wad of paper. At no time must any part of his foot come into contact with the ground.

Chariot Race In this race each team consists not of two players but of three. The 'horse' stands erect. Behind him the 'chariot' bends forward, placing his head in the small of the horse's back, and grasping the horse around the waist. The 'driver' of the chariot then mounts the chariot's back, holding the horse by the shoulders. In this position the teams race for the winning post.

Mini-Olympics

If you have a collection of gold, silver, and red milk-bottle tops, to serve as gold, silver, and bronze medals, that is fine. If not, any assortment of bottle-caps or similar articles will do for the awards in staging a mini-Olympics.

Sprint A 50-yard course is probably long enough for a family sprint, with first, second, and third home being awarded gold, silver, and bronze medals respectively.

Hurdles It is most unlikely that you will have any real hurdles to hand, but a hurdle may be simulated by scratching on the ground two parallel lines across the course, marking a gap of about 6 feet over which the runners must leap. A number of such hurdles about 5 or 6 yards apart should be drawn across the 60- or 80-yard course.

Long Jump A jumping line should be drawn on the ground, and each competitor should be allowed three attempts to see how far he can jump beyond it – the best of his three attempts being taken as his distance. There is no need to measure the distance jumped, unless a tape-measure happens to be to hand. A length of string or the edge of a towel can be laid down to show where a player has landed, and the string or towel can be moved forward to mark the new spot each time a jumper exceeds his own or someone else's previous effort.

High Jump Two fairly long sticks (about the length of broom-handles) should be held erect by two judges standing some 8 or 10 feet apart. The bottom ends of the sticks should be on the ground. A piece of string or coloured wool should then be stretched between the sticks and held tight, the judges holding it against the sticks by their thumbs. They should hold the string at a height which the competitor suggests he wants to try jumping. A competitor is entitled to go on raising the height on each attempt until he fouls the string. The height of successful jumps can be marked on the sticks with a pencil or thumb-nail scratch.

Javelin Practically any sort of stick 5 or 6 feet long will serve for a javelin-throwing contest, but all entrants must use the same stick. The person who throws it furthest is, of course, the winner. Make sure that the javelin is not thrown in the direction of any spectators.

Putting the Shot If you really want a trial of strength, select as the 'shot' a large, roundish stone weighing four or five pounds. If, on the other hand, you prefer a laugh, try putting the shot with something ridiculously light such as a balloon or ping-pong ball.

Discus A plastic plate will make a fine discus, provided there is plenty of open space and no danger of striking spectators – but remember that, if there is any wind about, a plastic plate may be carried dangerously off its course. In any case, it is just as much fun to use the cardboard top of an ice-cream tub (or even a playing card) to represent the discus. In this case the 'discus' should be held between the middle and index fingers, and flicked away.

Marathon For this event one needs a short but steep hill, or a stretch of extremely soft, dry sand on which running is difficult. Competitors then have to run to and fro the whole length of the course ten times. Anyone staggering to his knees is disqualified. If everyone collapses, the last to keel over is the winner.

In deciding the overall winner, each gold medal counts as three points, each silver as two, and each bronze as one. The contestant with the highest aggregate of points is presented with a cup – of water! He will probably need it!

Letting Off Steam

Boisterous pastimes for athletic youngsters who feel the need to work off excess energy.

Step On It

A piece of newspaper about 12 inches square is tied to a piece of string, wool, or cotton. The other end of the string is attached to the player's waist in such a way that the piece of paper trails on the ground about 3 feet behind him.

When all the players have each been thus equipped

with a tail, they stand in as large a ring as is reasonably possible within the space available. On the word 'Go!', they set off to chase one another, the object being to step on some other player's 'tail', thus ripping it off.

As soon as any portion of his tail is torn off in this way, that player must retire from the game, which proceeds until only one player is left with his tail intact. The players can then, if they so wish, make new tails and start all over again.

Under no circumstances is a player allowed to touch with his hands either his own tail or the tail of any other player.

Tilting

Each of the two contestants is equipped with two large spoons, one of which he holds in one hand and one in the other. In the left-hand spoon he balances an orange,

golf-ball, or similarly shaped object. With his other spoon he then tries to dislodge the orange (or whatever it is) that his opponent is balancing.

The winner is the player who first gains three falls in a row.

Jousting

In days of old when knights were bold, they endeavoured to dislodge one another from their steeds with lances. This is an amusing and surprisingly realistic imitation of that ancient sport.

The two opposing 'knights' face one another at a distance of about 10 or 15 feet, each standing on his right leg and holding his left ankle in his left hand. His right arm is extended straight forward as though it were a lance.

On the order 'Charge!', the knights hop towards one another in such a way that each will pass the other on his 'lance-side'. As they pass, each endeavours to knock his adversary off balance by placing his arm against the other's body and heaving clockwise. Striking with the arm is forbidden – the opponent must be thrown by a legitimate *heave*. Clinching is also forbidden.

If neither falls on the first 'pass', both must continue hopping five paces before turning and hopping back for a second pass.

The winner is, of course, the knight who causes his opponent to fall over.

Cock Fighting

A stretch of sand or a patch of soft grass is best for staging this contest which is really only suitable for four people who enjoy a rough-and-tumble. The fight is between two teams, each team being made up of two people, one of whom is carried pickaback.

The object of each team is now to pull the other team down. Punching or kicking is, of course, strictly forbidden, but any other clinch may be used in an effort to dislodge the opposing rider. If any part of the rider touches the ground that counts as a 'fall'. After a fall, each rider changes places with his mount for a return bout.

Blind Man's Duel

The two duellists are blindfolded, and each is given a rolled up newspaper as a sabre. They are then required to stalk one another with the object of landing hits on the opponent with the sabre.

Immediately before making a swipe, a duellist must first strike the palm of his own free hand with his sabre, as a warning sound for his opponent to duck or sidestep if he can. The striking of the palm preparatory to swiping is a rule to be strictly observed, and a player who has been hit cannot swipe back until he has first struck his own palm in accordance with the rule.

A third person should be available to act as referee, not only to settle disputed strikes, but also to warn the duellists if they are wandering out of reasonable range of one another, or moving towards some obstruction over which they might stumble.

Chinese Boxing

This is an amusing and perfectly safe trial of strength between two young and evenly matched opponents, but it is probably more a boys' game than a girls'.

The two contestants stand facing one another, their fingers interlocked with their opponent's fingers, palm to palm. The bout starts by the boxers extending their left arms, with their right arms held back against their shoulders.

On the bell being sounded (by the referee banging a can or calling 'Dong') each strives to strike his opponent's left shoulder – which can only be done by forcing the opponent to bend his left arm.

After a successful hit, the boxers resume their original stance for a second round, but this time they commence with their left arms bent, and their right arms extended for an attempt to strike the opponent's right shoulder. The first boxer to gain three hits on his opponent's shoulder wins the match.

Chinese Wrestling is another way for energetic youngsters to let off steam, but it should preferably be played on ground which provides a soft fall.

The wrestlers stand back-to-back, and with their arms swung back to encircle one another's waist. Alternatively they may link themselves together back-to-back by hooking their elbows together.

From this position each tries to throw the other off-balance. If any part of a wrestler's body with the exception of his feet touches the ground, that counts as a fall against him. Once again, the first wrestler to gain three falls is the winner of the match.

Running the Gauntlet

This game is usually popular with those who like to expose themselves to danger. Though it can be played with as few as three, it is more fun with a larger party of perhaps eight or ten.

One player is chosen to run the gauntlet, the others dividing themselves into two equal lines about 8 feet apart (i.e. about twice the distance of an extended arm plus a towel length). These players should space themselves about 5 feet apart from their neighbours in the line, and each should be equipped with a towel.

The remaining player's ordeal is now to 'run the gauntlet' between the two lines, while the others (without moving from their places) strive to flick the runner with the ends of their towels.

If the lines are too far apart, strikes are impossible.

If they are too close together, they are virtually inevitable, hence the necessity to keep a strict distance, for which skill and timing is required by both the runner and the whippers.

Eve-a-Nodding

The players are divided into two equal teams, and take their places behind two parallel lines drawn on the ground about 20 yards apart. One team is designated 'odds', and the other team 'evens'.

An independent umpire then commences counting very slowly, 'One ... two ... three ... four ...' etc. He must count loudly and clearly, and, above all, at a steady, *even* rate.

As he counts, the two teams creep towards one another – until without warning the umpire stops counting.

If the last number he has said before stopping was an odd number, the odds must dash forward in an attempt to tag the evens before the evens can get back behind their own base line. Any even who is tagged before crossing his home line henceforth becomes an odd and plays with the team of his former opponents.

If the last number called by the umpire was even, it is of course the evens who become the pursuers, and the odds the fugitives.

The game continues until all players belong to a single team, the other team having been completely exterminated.

Snatch and Grab

Two circles each about 10 feet in diameter and separated from one another by about 10 yards are scratched out on the ground, and the players are divided into two equal teams. One team is called 'snatch', and the other team 'grab'.

The game begins by all the players forming a circle in the middle of the pitch, and by someone tossing a scarf, towel, or similar piece of material into the air. As soon as a player gains possession of the scarf he cries out the name of his team, 'Snatch' or 'Grab', whereupon all members of his team must commence hopping on the *right* leg (grasping the left ankle with the left hand) and all the members of the opposing team must hop on the *left* leg (holding the right ankle with the right hand).

The opposing team must then try to snatch or grab the scarf from whichever player is holding it. The scarf must always be held at arm's length, and if it is clutched, the player who was holding it must let it go immediately.

As soon as another player gains possession of the scarf he cries out the name of his team, whereupon all players have to hop on the other foot. This means that the team in possession of the scarf is always hopping on the right foot, and the one pursuing the scarf on the left foot. In this way the player with the scarf can identify friend from foe in the event of his wanting to pass the scarf or throw it if he is in danger of being cornered.

A goal is scored by the player who successfully carries the scarf into his own team's home circle.

Five minutes of this exhausting sport is usually enough for most players, after which the umpire should call 'Half Time' – or 'Full Time' if most of the players have collapsed.

Go-getters

This game has been played down through the ages under a variety of names and is perhaps the most effective way of reducing an excess energy level.

A semicircle about 10 feet in diameter is scratched out, preferably against some hedge, fence, or cliff-face, and around some tree or rock which can serve as a landmark. This area is called 'the gaol'.

The players then divide into two equal teams called the 'goers' and the 'getters'.

At the beginning of the game the goers scatter, and the getters pursue them with the object of tagging them. When a getter tags one of his opponents' he cries 'Get!', whereupon the tagged player must surrender and allow himself to be escorted back to the gaol by his captor.

A goer must remain in gaol until one of his own team

manages to run through the gaol without he himself being tagged. If a free goer manages to get even one foot within any part of the semicircle he is entitled to cry 'Go!' All the imprisoned goers are by this act released, and once again scatter.

The game concludes when all the goers have been captured, and none remains to liberate his team-mates. The teams then swap roles for a return contest – that is, if anyone has any energy left. If they haven't, they had better turn back to an earlier page of this book, and settle for something less strenuous!

THE PUFFIN MONSTER JOKE BOOK
Martyn Forrester

A fun book of jokes about monsters, vampires, and other horrors, suitably illustrated by David McKee.

LAUGH YOUR HEAD OFF!
Martyn Forrester

A collection of hysterical and historical jokes and facts. Did you know that the French eat about five hundred million snails a year? Or that Louis XIV had only three baths in his whole life?

THE PUFFIN TRIVIA QUIZGAME BOOK

A mind-boggling collection of Trivia questions plus games for the younger members of the family.

PETS FOR KEEPS
Dick King-Smith

Twelve simple pets, from hamsters to budgies, each with an anecdote, and lots of useful and practical hints for pet owners and potential owners.

THE PUFFIN BOOK OF
BRAINTEASERS

Eric Emmet

A collection of original puzzles ranging from simple addition and division problems through football and cricket puzzles, and the adventures of Professor Knowall and Sergeant Simple, to the curious habits of Wotta-Woppas and the Shilla-Shallas on the Island of Imperfection. None of the problems require any specialist mathematical knowledge and they are arranged in order of difficulty. For each one there is a completely explained solution and there are Hints and Suggestions on how to set about solving them and reaching the correct answer.

THE PUFFIN BOOK OF
INDOOR GAMES

Andrew Pennycook

A stimulating selection of games, 75 in all, divided into six main areas: card games, dominoes, board games, dice, pencil and paper games, and match games. Graded in difficulty within each section with clear explanations, helpful diagrams and amusing cartoons, this will be the ideal book for those at a loose end and for those who simply love games.

THE CRACK-A-JOKE BOOK

The 1,000th Puffin and a special book of jokes sent to the Goodies by children. For children of all ages.

THE END

Richard Stanley

Packed full of the best worst jokes, loathsome limericks and pathetic poems, this book is a groan-a-minute.

HOW TO SURVIVE
Brian Hildreth

Everything you need to know about surviving in a hostile environment – how to build fires and shelters, how to find food and water, vital first aid and herbal remedies, how to read a map and use the International Code of Signals. All these things, and many more, provide a very useful handbook. Illustrated in black and white.

TOWN WATCH
COUNTRY WATCH
Dick King-Smith

Two books taking an informative look at the natural world and finding out about animals in the world around us.

THE CHRISTMAS STOCKING JOKE BOOK
Shoo Rayner

Laugh your Christmas stockings off with this cracker of a joke book. Bursting with hilarious fun, this collection of Christmas jokes and cartoons will keep you and your family laughing all the way through from Christmas Eve to the New Year!

THE PUFFIN BOOK OF
HANDWRITING
Tom Gourdie

Write an alphabet in a tree of hearts, fill in word puzzles, trace letters, draw line patterns, have fun and acquire an elegant style of handwriting.

THE ANIMAL QUIZ BOOK
Sally Kilroy

An extensively illustrated quiz book covering all kinds of animals, birds, insects and reptiles. The first sections of the book are general ones, i.e. quizzes about the proper names for animal homes, animal young, masculine/feminine, markings and camouflage, countries of origin, biggest-smallest-fastest, etc. Later sections refer to specific animals, i.e. everything you could want to know about an elephant.

Johnny Ball's THINK BOX and SECOND THINKS

Johnny Ball, whose TV shows have made maths a popular subject with millions of children, shares his enthusiasm for numbers in these fascinating books of puzzles, tricks and brain teasers.

THE JOKE BOX
Gyles Brandreth

A serious but at the same time hilarious guide to being funny. Full of examples which cannot fail to entertain.

PUZZLER'S A to Z
Colin Grumbrell

Puzzle your way from A to Z with these inventive and entertaining anagrams, word searches, shape and number puzzles, crosswords and quizzes of all kinds.